HERTFORD LOOP

Vic Mitchell and Keith Smith

Middleton Press

Front cover: A Moorgate to Cuffley train is about to leave Palmers Green in about 1920. No. 1561 is displaying its massive condensing pipe used in the tunnels to Moorgate to avoid emitting steam. (R.M.Casserley coll.)

Back cover: Recorded on 2nd February 2009 is Sopers Viaduct, which is south of Cuffley and north of the M25 bridge. The train is the 11.50 Letchworth to Moorgate and is formed of two three-car class 313 units. (P.Dace)

> **This album is published to mark the centenary of the opening of the Enfield to Cuffley line in 1910.**

Published March 2010

ISBN 978 1 906008 71 0

© Middleton Press, 2010

Design Deborah Esher

Published by
    Middleton Press
    Easebourne Lane
    Midhurst
    West Sussex
    GU29 9AZ
Tel: 01730 813169
Fax: 01730 812601
Email: info@middletonpress.co.uk
www.middletonpress.co.uk

Printed in the United Kingdom by Henry Ling Limited, at the Dorset Press, Dorchester, DT1 1HD

INDEX

78	Bayford	85	Hertford North
10	Bounds Green Depot	19	Palmers Green
12	Bowes Park	104	Stapleford
60	Crews Hill	116	Stevenage
65	Cuffley	107	Watton-at-Stone
36	Enfield Chase	26	Winchmore Hill
45	Gordon Hill	1	Wood Green
31	Grange Park		

ACKNOWLEDGEMENTS

We are very grateful for the assistance received from many of those mentioned in the credits also to A.R.Carder, L.Crosier, G.Croughton, T.Hancock, P.Hodge, S.C.Jenkins, N.Langridge, Mr D. and Dr S.Salter, T.Walsh and in particular, our always supportive wives, Barbara Mitchell and Janet Smith. The librarians at the Institute of Civil Engineers have kindly supplied copies of the construction photographs.

I. Route diagram for the 1930s.

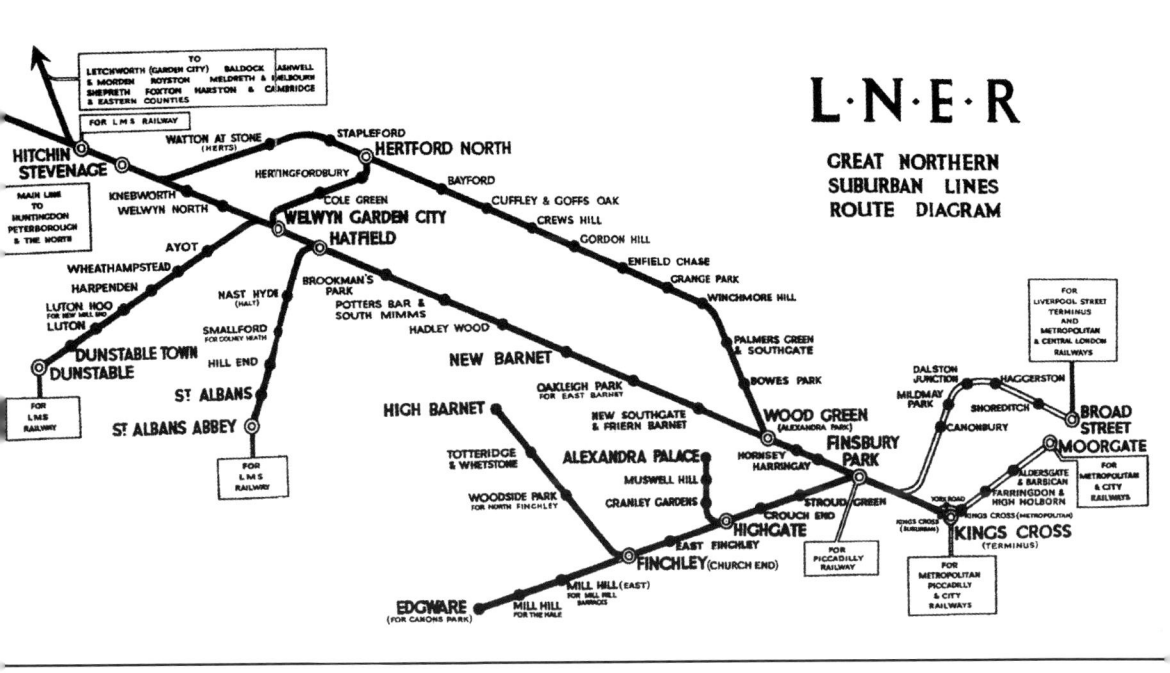

GEOGRAPHICAL SETTING

The route northwards to Enfield is now urban, but was rural when it was built. It was the prime cause of this development and the underlying London clay was used for the necessary brick production.

The long established market town of Hertford is situated near to where the Rivers Mimram, Rib and Beane join the Lea. We pass over two south of Hertford North and the last one north thereof (twice).

The climb out of London lasts nine miles and ends at Ponsbourne Tunnel. A much shorter descent to Hertford follows. The remainder of the route traverses the chalk of the dip slope of the northern extension of the Chiltern Hills.

The route was constructed in the counties of Middlesex and Hertfordshire, the boundary being just north of Crews Hill.

The maps are to the scale of 25ins to 1 mile, with north at the top unless otherwise indicated.

Hertford Loop Gradient Profile.

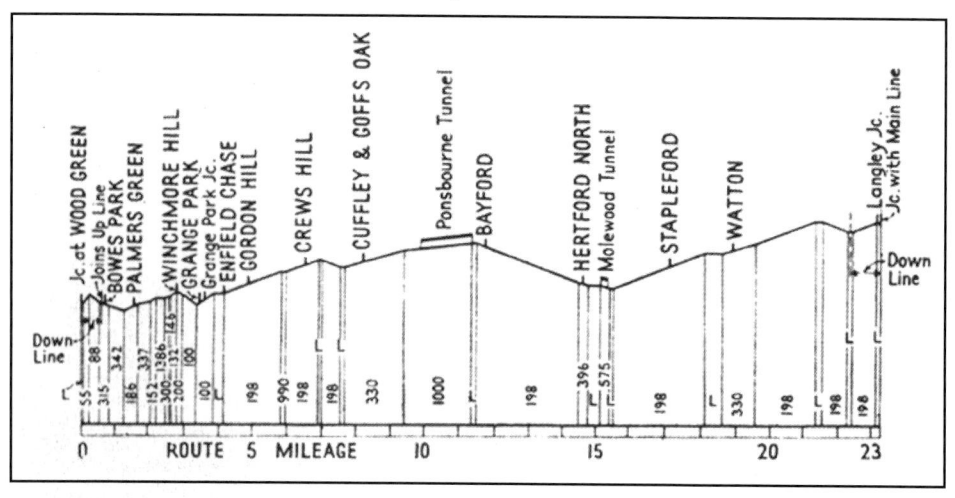

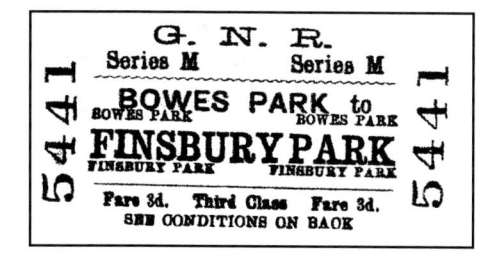

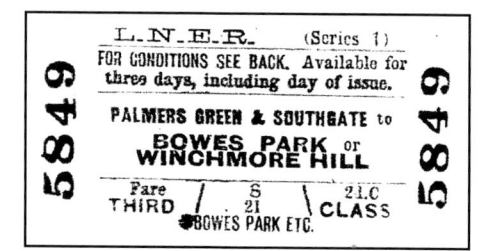

HISTORICAL BACKGROUND

Hertford received its first trains on a branch line from Broxbourne in October 1843. This became part of the Great Eastern Railway in 1862.

A branch from the west followed on 1st March 1858, when trains began running from Hatfield, on the Great Northern Railway's main line of 1850. This company began to develop its suburban network by opening a branch from its main line at Wood Green, northwards to Enfield, on 1st April 1871. The Hornsey & Hertford Railway Act had been passed in 1865.

The Enfield-Stevenage line was authorised in 1898 and GNR services to Cuffley began on 4th April 1910. Freight traffic started between Cuffley and Stevenage on 4th March 1918, although part was only single line until 23rd December 1920. The Hertford Loop soon served as an important diversionary route for all types of train. Local services to Stevenage began on it on 2nd June 1924, when a new station at Hertford North came into use. However, trains were sparse north thereof and were suspended from 11th September 1939 until 4th March 1962.

The GNR and GER had become part of the new London & North Eastern Railway in 1923. This largely formed the Eastern Region of British Railways upon nationalisation in 1948. The story of the various stations in Hertford is told in detail in that section of this volume.

Closures began on 1st October 1951, when passenger service was curtailed between Hertford and St. Albans. Goods facilities were withdrawn at most locations on the route in 1962-65. Details are in the captions.

Full electric services on the Hertford East line began on 21st November 1960, the current being 25kV AC. The same applied at Hertford North from 8th November 1976, but only southwards. Electric services northwards began on 6th February 1978.

West Anglia Great Northern or WAGN was that part of Prism Rail which received a 7¼ year franchise from 5th January 1997, following privatisation. WAGN was merged with Thameslink in April 2006, to form First Capital Connect.

The prolonged construction period was photographed at intervals. This view from its early years is of the north portal of Molewood Tunnel, about one mile north of Hertford. (ICE)

PASSENGER SERVICES
South of Hertford

The line opened to Enfield with a service of 16 weekday trains and five on Sundays. The later weekday numbers varied. For example, it was 55 in 1903, 80 in the early 1930s and 42 in 1951, with 14 more as far as Gordon Hill on work days. Most trains had run to Hertford North from 1924.

Most originated at King's Cross, although a few started at Finsbury Park. Peak hour services served Moorgate, trains using the outer platforms at King's Cross. However, in the early years, a few GNR services originated at Victoria, ran via Brixton and Farringdon Street, throughout the week. Broad Street also became an important peak hour terminus, the service being provided by the North London Railway initially.

The South Eastern Railway ran trains from Woolwich to Finsbury Park from 1878 and they were later extended to Enfield, but ceased in 1907.

Electrification meant that almost all trains originated at Moorgate from November 1976, but they ran in the former Northern City tube tunnels and thus did not call at King's Cross. They were dual voltage EMUs, as 750 volts DC was used underground. There were three each hour on weekdays and two on Sundays.

North of Hertford

The service on this section was independent of that southwards for many decades. Initially the four weekday trains ran to Hitchin; there were none on Sundays. A railcar was provided in the early 1930s and there were five trips by 1935. Service ceased with the advent of World War II.

Restoration came on 5th March 1962, but with just two trains in the peak hours and hourly on Saturdays. They were DMUs. There were eight trips in 1974 and 12 in 1977, weekdays only. From May 1982, an amazing 18 trains ran between Moorgate and Letchworth on weekdays, with 16 on Sundays.

1873

1926

1938

1890

1911

1925

WOOD GREEN

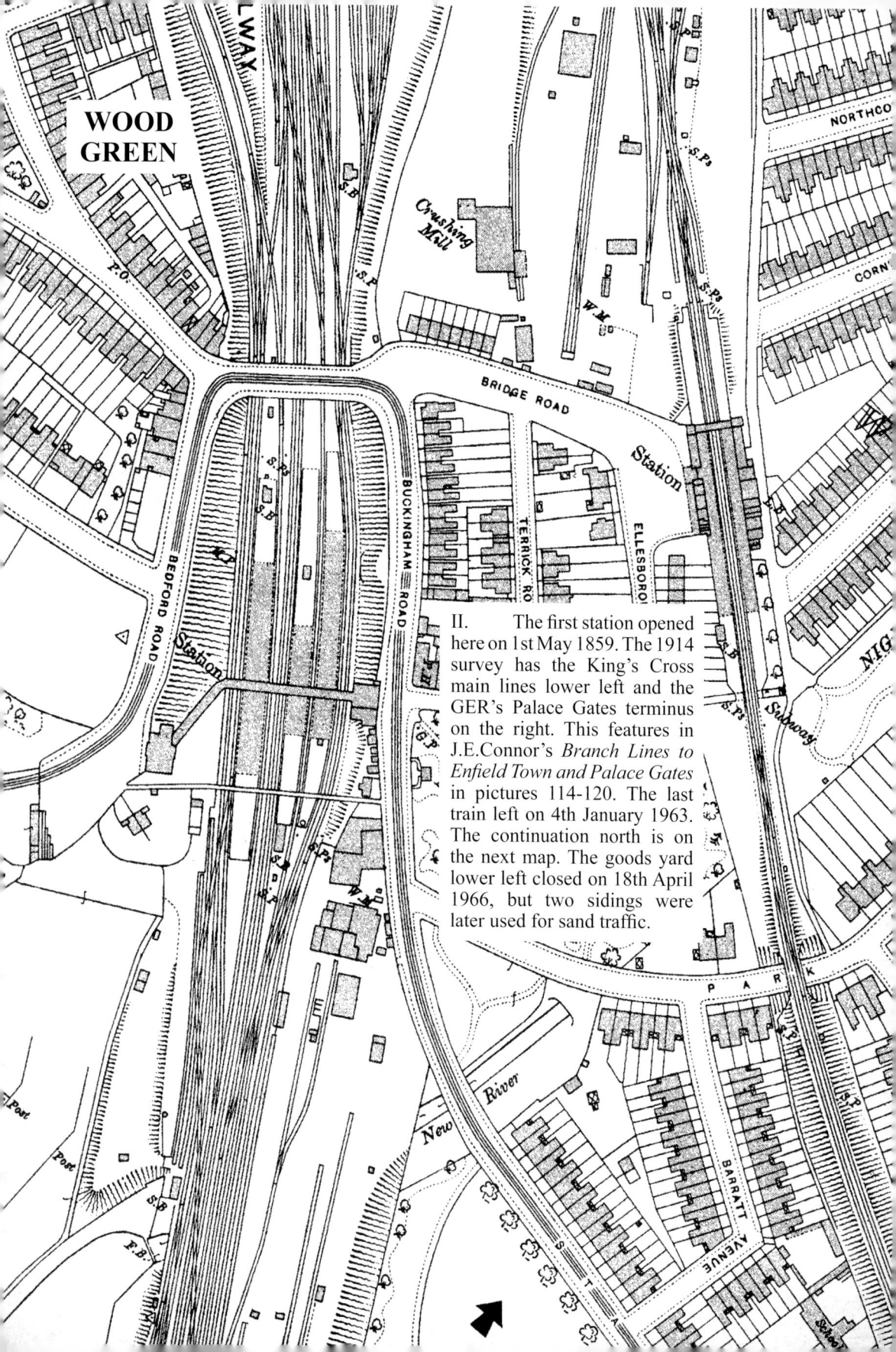

II. The first station opened here on 1st May 1859. The 1914 survey has the King's Cross main lines lower left and the GER's Palace Gates terminus on the right. This features in J.E.Connor's *Branch Lines to Enfield Town and Palace Gates* in pictures 114-120. The last train left on 4th January 1963. The continuation north is on the next map. The goods yard lower left closed on 18th April 1966, but two sidings were later used for sand traffic.

1. The simple country station with two short platforms was replaced by three island platforms in 1871, when the route from King's Cross was quadrupled and the Enfield branch came into use. Its down trains used the western platform and the up services used the one on the far left. The down booking office is on the right. The 1887 Down Box No. 3 is also on the right.
(Lens of Sutton coll.)

2. The nearest platform face was used by up trains from Enfield and is featured in another Edwardian postcard. The footbridge in the background was added in 1910. (Lens of Sutton coll.)

3. Two photographs from 4th October 1957 feature expresses speeding through. Alongside the fogmans hut is no. 60059 *Tracery*, a class A3 with double blastpipe and chimney. (H.Ballantyne)

4. The 2.45pm King's Cross to Newcastle is headed by no. 60866, a class V2 2-6-2 design introduced by Gresley in 1936. The signal box is Up Box No. 4. (H.Ballantyne)

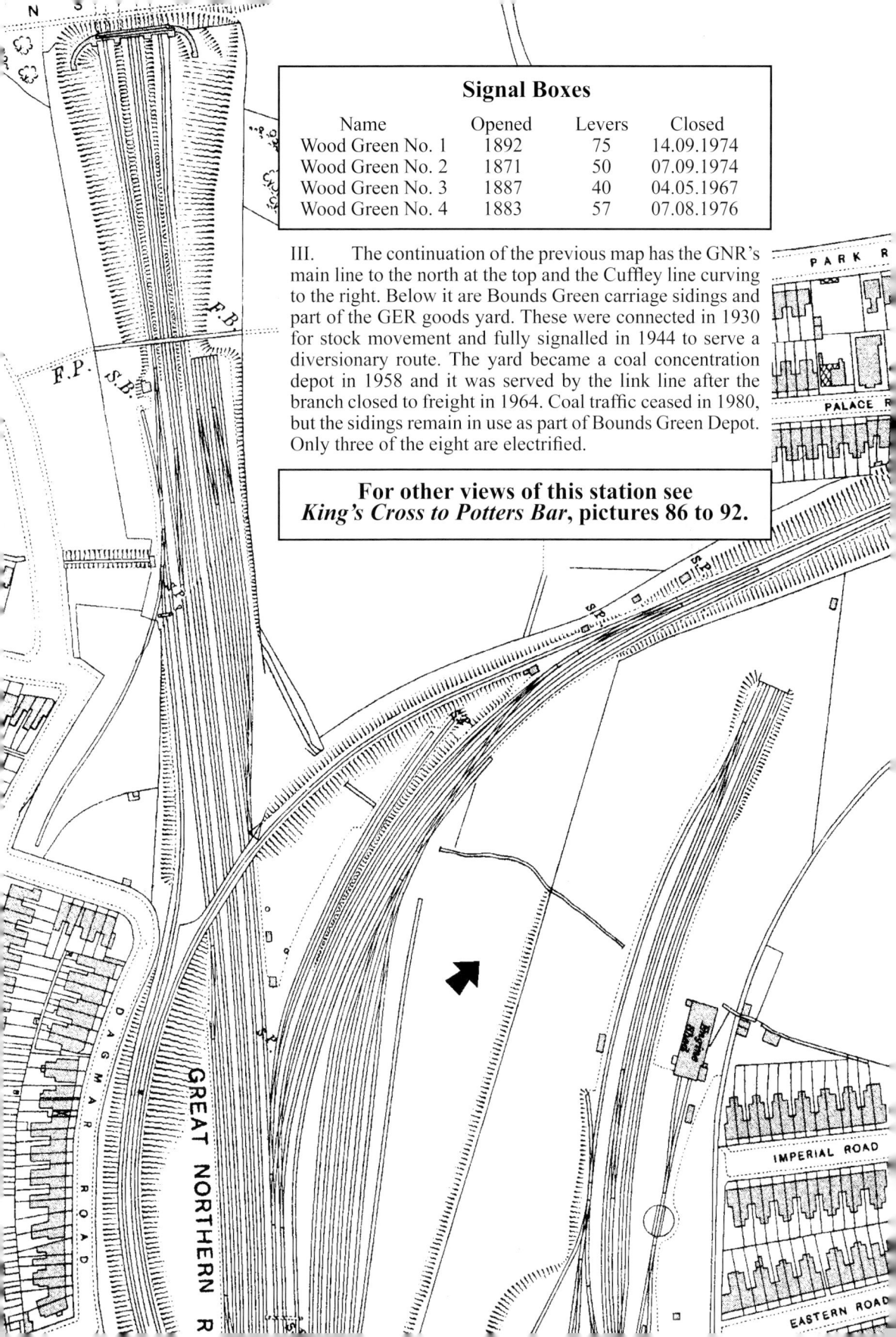

Signal Boxes

Name	Opened	Levers	Closed
Wood Green No. 1	1892	75	14.09.1974
Wood Green No. 2	1871	50	07.09.1974
Wood Green No. 3	1887	40	04.05.1967
Wood Green No. 4	1883	57	07.08.1976

III.   The continuation of the previous map has the GNR's main line to the north at the top and the Cuffley line curving to the right. Below it are Bounds Green carriage sidings and part of the GER goods yard. These were connected in 1930 for stock movement and fully signalled in 1944 to serve a diversionary route. The yard became a coal concentration depot in 1958 and it was served by the link line after the branch closed to freight in 1964. Coal traffic ceased in 1980, but the sidings remain in use as part of Bounds Green Depot. Only three of the eight are electrified.

**For other views of this station see
King's Cross to Potters Bar, pictures 86 to 92.**

5. The down fast line is seen again, it being the centre one in this northward view from about 1960. Its relaying with flat-bottom rail has severed the staff crossing. The nearest bridge carries a public footpath. (Lens of Sutton coll.)

6. Moving north on the same day, we note that the road bridge widening had been undertaken with flat spans; much quicker than brick laying. In the distance is the southern extremity of Bounds Green Depot.
(Lens of Sutton coll.)

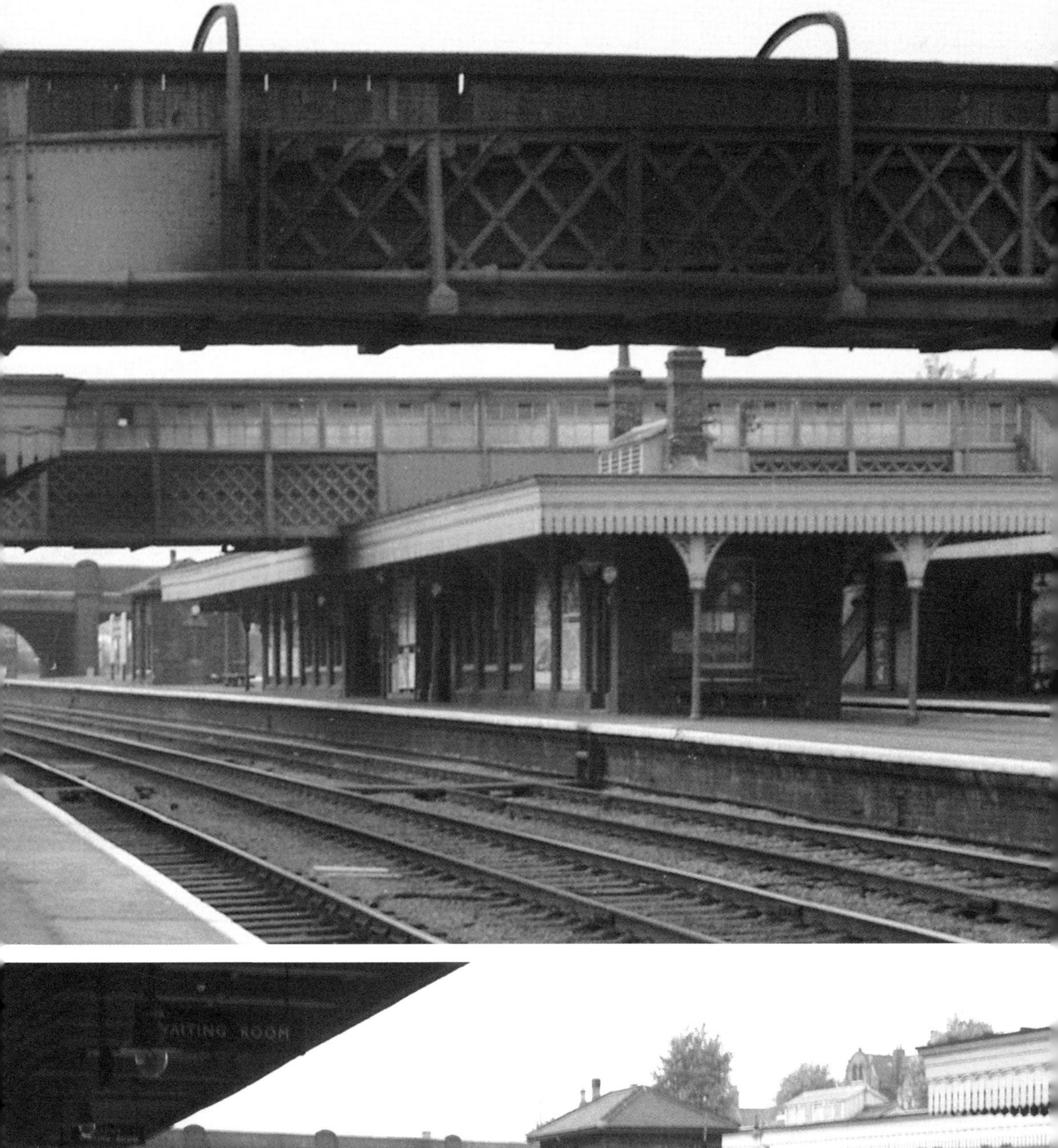

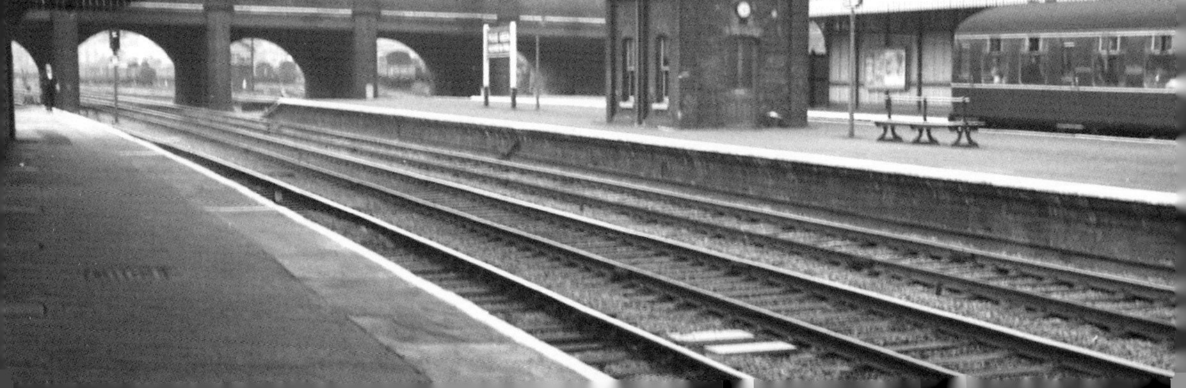

7. Up Box No. 4 was recorded on 27th March 1971, along with a notable variety of signal posts. (E.Wilmshurst)

For an alternative light rail journey northwards, see *Enfield and Wood Green Tramways* (Middleton Press).

8. The suffix "Alexandra Park" was used between 1864 and March 1971, but was not universally applied. This is the up side booking office on 2nd March 1982, two weeks before the station was renamed "Alexandra Palace". The palace itself had housed Britain's first TV station and had then been recently renovated for public events. (D.A.Thompson)

9. All the buildings, except the up booking office, were demolished in 1974. The down side one had been closed in 1967, following slippage of the bank on the left. This also meant the loss of the down goods line. (D.A.Thompson)

BOUNDS GREEN DEPOT

10. A northward panorama through arches seen in picture 6 includes much of the depot site in May 1971. It had started as two sidings when the Enfield branch opened and had grown to 12 by 1913. In the left background is the flyover provided for branch down trains when the line opened. It is thus one of the oldest. The signal box is Wood Green Up Box No.2. (Milepost 92½)

11. This westward view from 24th April 1988 has the tower used for early TV output in the background, Alexandra Palace being on a hill. Centre is the six-road servicing shed and behind the locomotives is the two-road repair shed. There are five sidings near the coaches and beyond them are the Up Hertford and the Avoiding lines. (A.C.Mott)

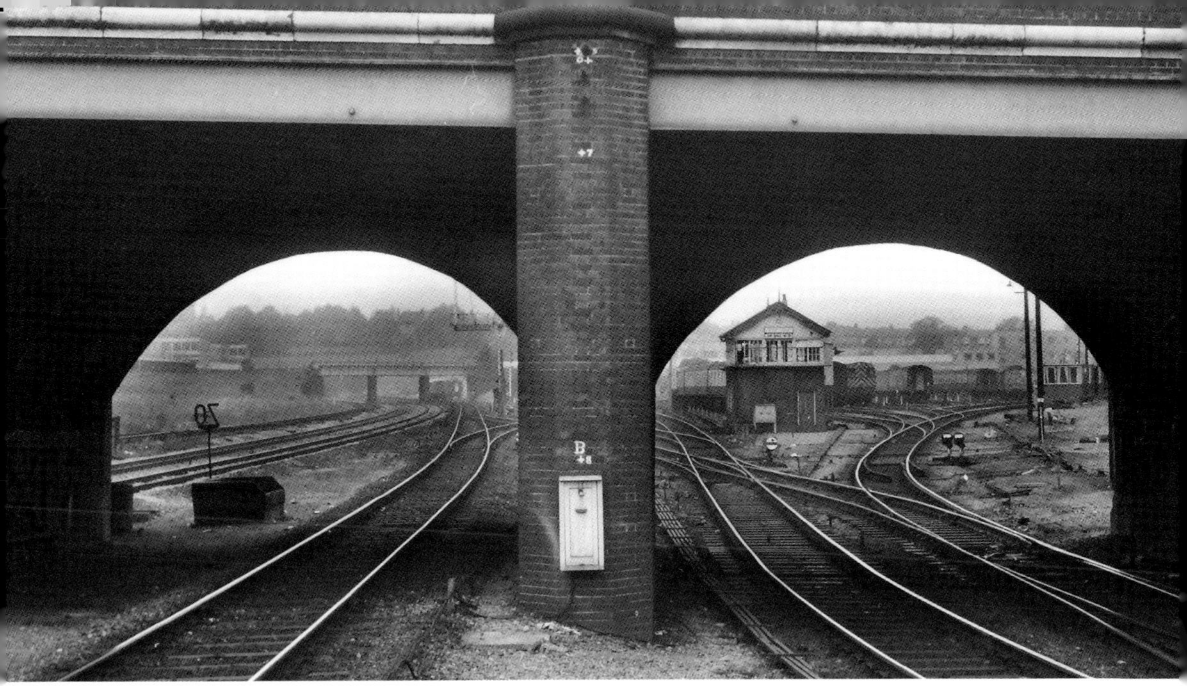
+7
B
+8

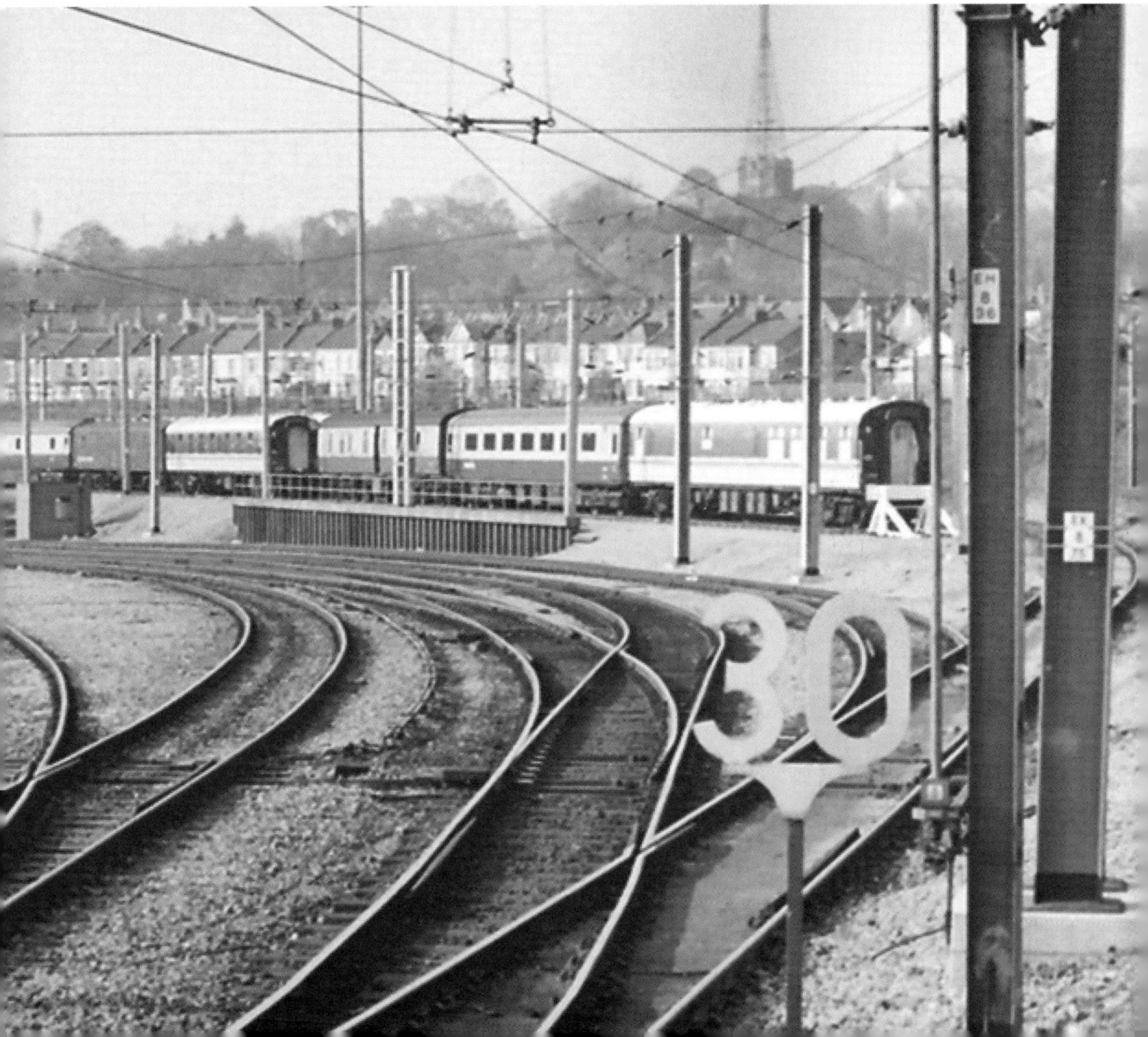
30

BOWES PARK

IV. The 1914 survey includes the reversing siding. This and the lower crossover were later electrified and were still in use in 2010.

12. Two Edwardian postcards set the scene. Part of the booking office shown spans an up train in this view. The sloping roof to the right of it is over the steps down to Station Road. (Lens of Sutton coll.)

13. All wearing the correct hats for their station in life, a group wait for an up train to stop behind a well-coaled tank engine. The way out involved two reversed flights of stairs. (Lens of Sutton coll.)

14. Here we look towards Wood Green in the 1950s, probably after the demolition of the signal box, although it had been disused for many years. (Lens of Sutton coll.)

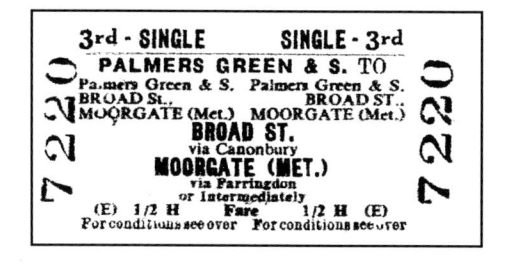

15. At the other end of the platform, improvements were in progress in the 1960s. The booking office and the footbridge were demolished prior to electrification. They would have been too close to the wires. (Lens of Sutton coll.)

16. The London end of the station was recorded on 1st April 1961. The signals are for the two lines mentioned at the end of caption 11. At that time there were no trains starting here. There was a signal box with 20 levers from 1880 to 1942. (B.W.L.Brooksbank)

17. The new footbridge was devoid of a roof, but at least one was provided over the steps for the benefit of travellers in the snow. The entrance is seen in 1989; the new ticket office was built on the platform. A new and longer bridge had been built over the nearby North Circular Road in 1965. (D.A.Thompson)

18. EMU no. 317335 arrives on 9th May 1991, while working from Huntingdon to King's Cross. There was an hourly such service on Saturdays at that time; there were no trains to Moorgate at weekends. The siding was not used by terminating trains at that period, except in emergencies. (F.Hornby)

PALMERS GREEN

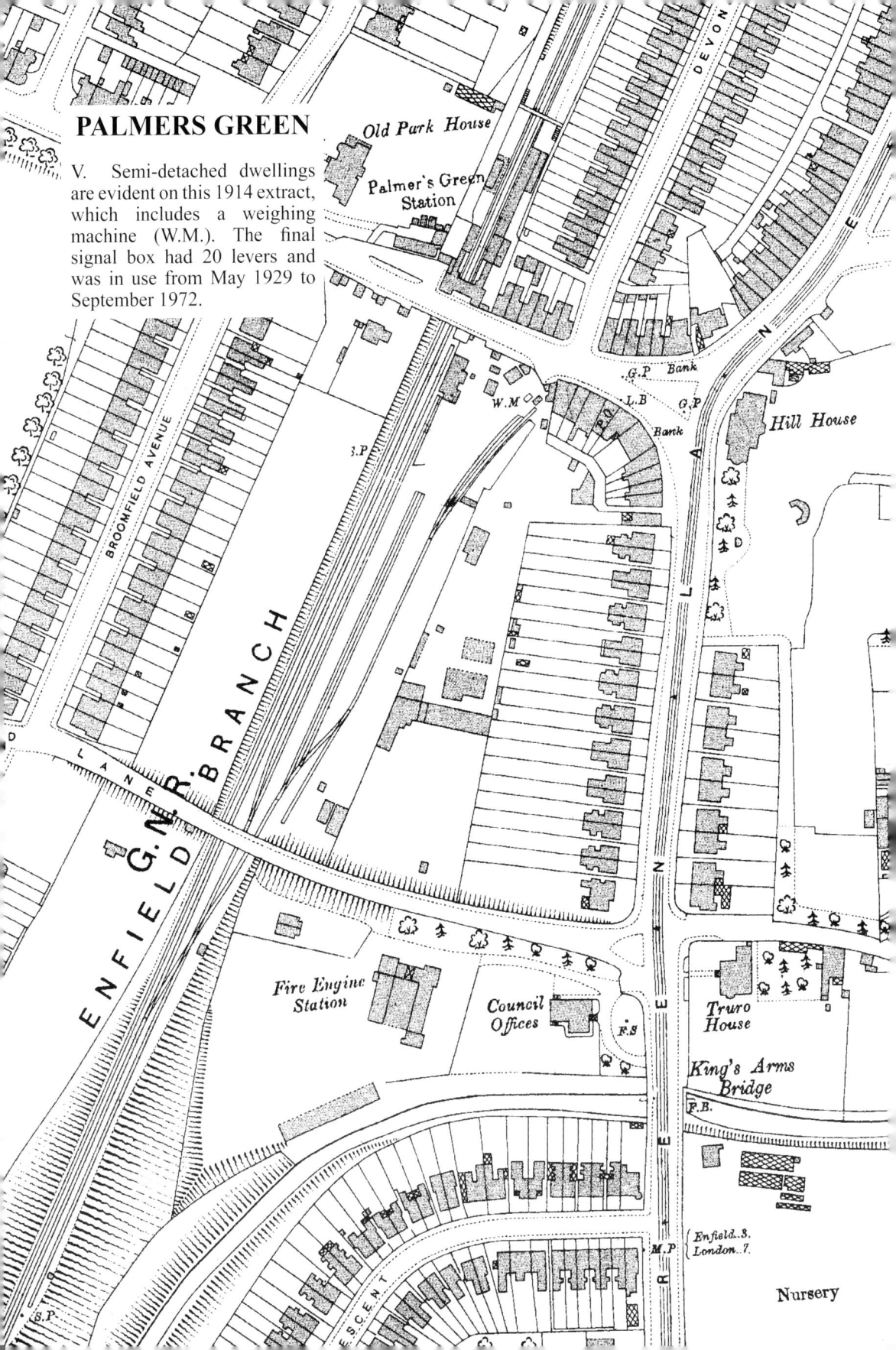

V. Semi-detached dwellings are evident on this 1914 extract, which includes a weighing machine (W.M.). The final signal box had 20 levers and was in use from May 1929 to September 1972.

19. Three Edwardian views create the early ambiance very well. On the left is the connecting bus to Southgate, an area that was not served by the Piccadilly Line until 1933. (Lens of Sutton coll.)

20. This is another station with its entrance at road level and steps down to the platform. A first generation motor bus approaches the younger generation of sail modellers, waiting on the bridge over the tracks. (Lens of Sutton coll.)

21. We look south from the down platform before the footbridge was built; it appears on the 1914 edition of the map. The tall building included shops, a bank and the post office on its other side. (Lens of Sutton coll.)

22. Class N2 0-6-2T no. 4741 departs north, probably in the 1930s. The coaches were known as Quad-Art: they had four bodies on five bogies. The term for the GNR signal was "Somersault". (J.Langford coll.)

23. The suffix shown on the running-in board was in use from 1876 until 1971. This southward view from the 1960s includes the goods yard, which was in use until 1st October 1962.
(Lens of Sutton coll.)

24. The modernised exterior was recorded on 22nd April 1987. The station had its best ever service with the advent of electrification. A sign of the times were bars at the windows.
(D.A.Thompson)

⬇ 25. No. 313020 is about to leave for King's Cross on 29th October 1994, amidst prodigious undergrowth. A notable loss was part of the down canopy; the footbridge also vanished. (F.Hornby)

WINCHMORE HILL

VI. This 1913 extract includes the small goods yard at the top. It was in use until 1st October 1962 and had a long sloping access lane from the main road.

26. The same basic design was employed at Palmers Green. The coal office was near the entrance; the same applied in picture 12 at Bowes Park. (Lens of Sutton coll.)

27. Similar canopies were provided at its southern neighbour but the toilets are on the platform. This may have been due to drainage constraints. Gas lighting was still in evidence in the early 1960s. There is a signal beyond the bridge; all arms were removed during World War II. (Lens of Sutton coll.)

28.   By the time the exterior was photographed on 22nd April 1987, the west wing had been lost, due to subsidence. The remainder of the structure had been renovated and conserved. The signal box had only eight levers and functioned from 1st April 1871 to 3rd September 1972. It was near the stairwell on the up platform. (D.A.Thompson)

29.   A fully glazed waiting shelter, with a pitched roof, was provided on the up platform. Approaching it on 22nd June 1987 is no. 313018, which is working from Letchworth to Moorgate. The collector shoe beam is evident on no. 313026, which is running to Letchworth. (B.Morrison)

30. No. 317369 is bound for King's Cross on 29th October 1994. The roofs over the stairs and the intervening windows have vanished. The windows were bricked up due to the proximity of the 25kV wires. (F.Hornby)

GRANGE PARK

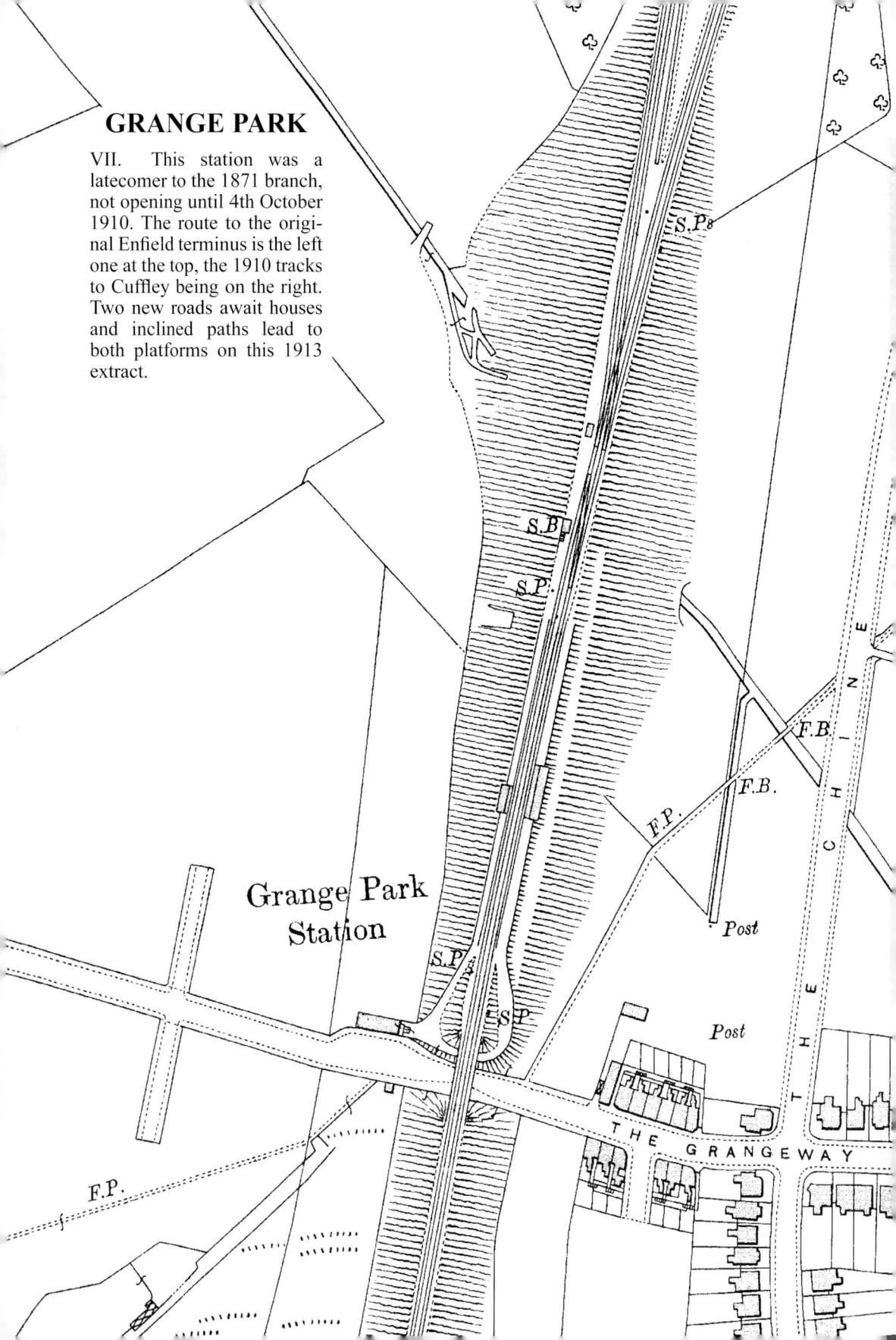

VII. This station was a latecomer to the 1871 branch, not opening until 4th October 1910. The route to the original Enfield terminus is the left one at the top, the 1910 tracks to Cuffley being on the right. Two new roads await houses and inclined paths lead to both platforms on this 1913 extract.

31.   Looking east, we find the booking office on the left and the path to the up platform passing under the left arch. (Lens of Sutton coll.)

32.   A down train approaches while the station was still gas lit in the 1960s. We have the opportunity to note that all the structures were of timber, this being to reduce the weight on the embankment. (Lens of Sutton coll.)

33. A northward panorama from 5th July 1971 includes a small signal arm for trains to Enfield goods yard, which was at the site of the original terminus. The 25-lever signal box served from 7th July 1909 to 3rd September 1972. The drilling rig was used for monitoring underground temperature as there was a subterrainian fire causing track settlement. London rubbish had been used in the construction of embankments and this always contained unburnt coal. (Milepost 92½)

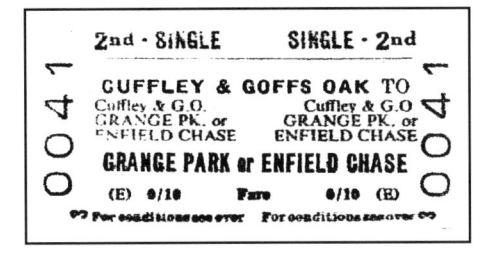

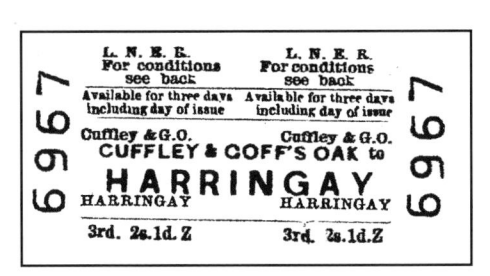

34.   This photograph is from 1st June 1996 and shows the situation after electric traction and electric lighting had been introduced. (R.Hummerston)

35.   A record from 11th March 1997 shows no. 313032 northbound, open plan shelters and the latest departure indicators. The 07.44 from Moorgate did not stop here, also the 16.05, 17.04, 17.34 and 18.04 ran through at that time. (F.Hornby)

NORTH OF GRANGE PARK

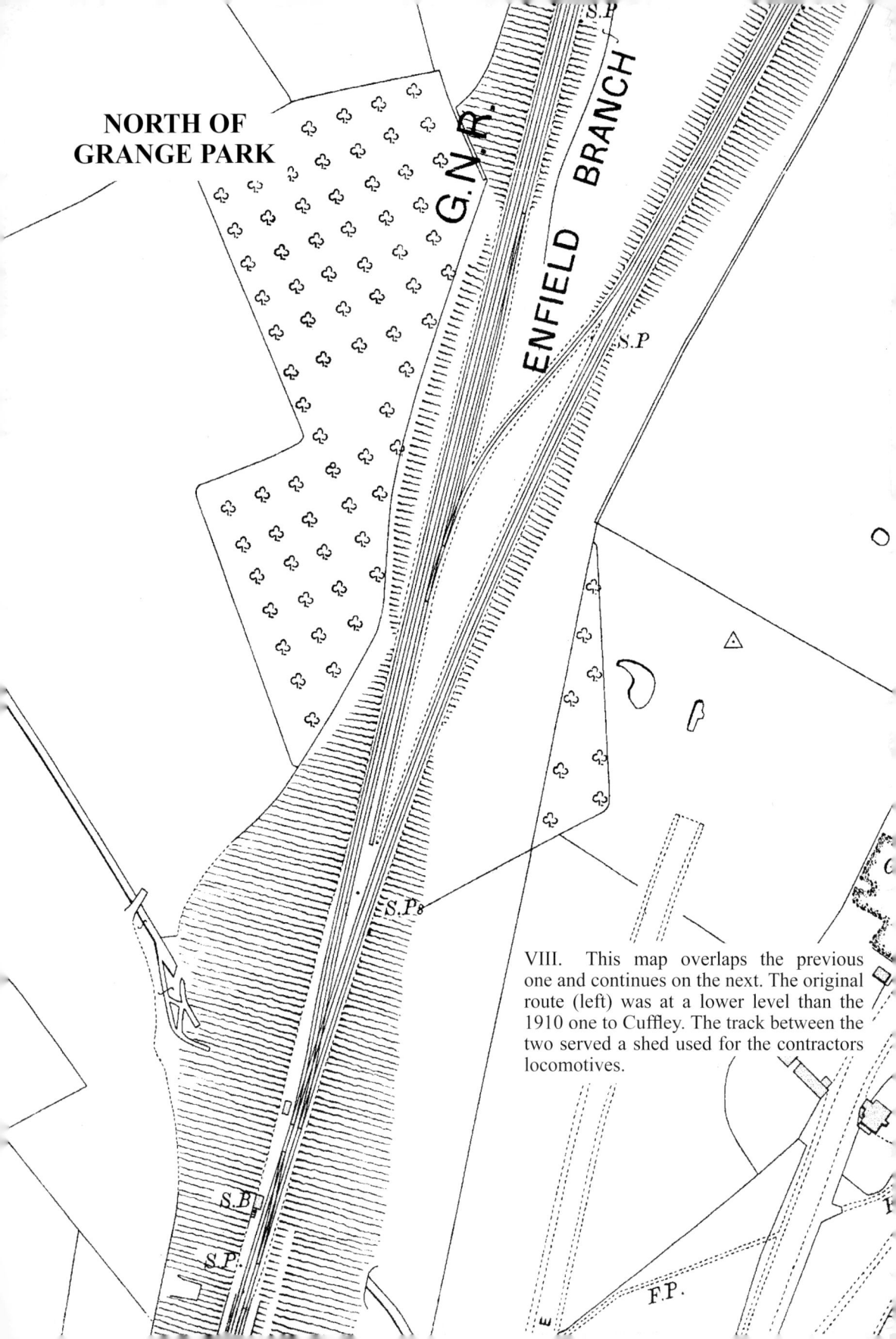

G.N.R.

ENFIELD BRANCH

S.P

S.P

S.P.

S.B.

S.P.

F.P.

VIII. This map overlaps the previous one and continues on the next. The original route (left) was at a lower level than the 1910 one to Cuffley. The track between the two served a shed used for the contractors locomotives.

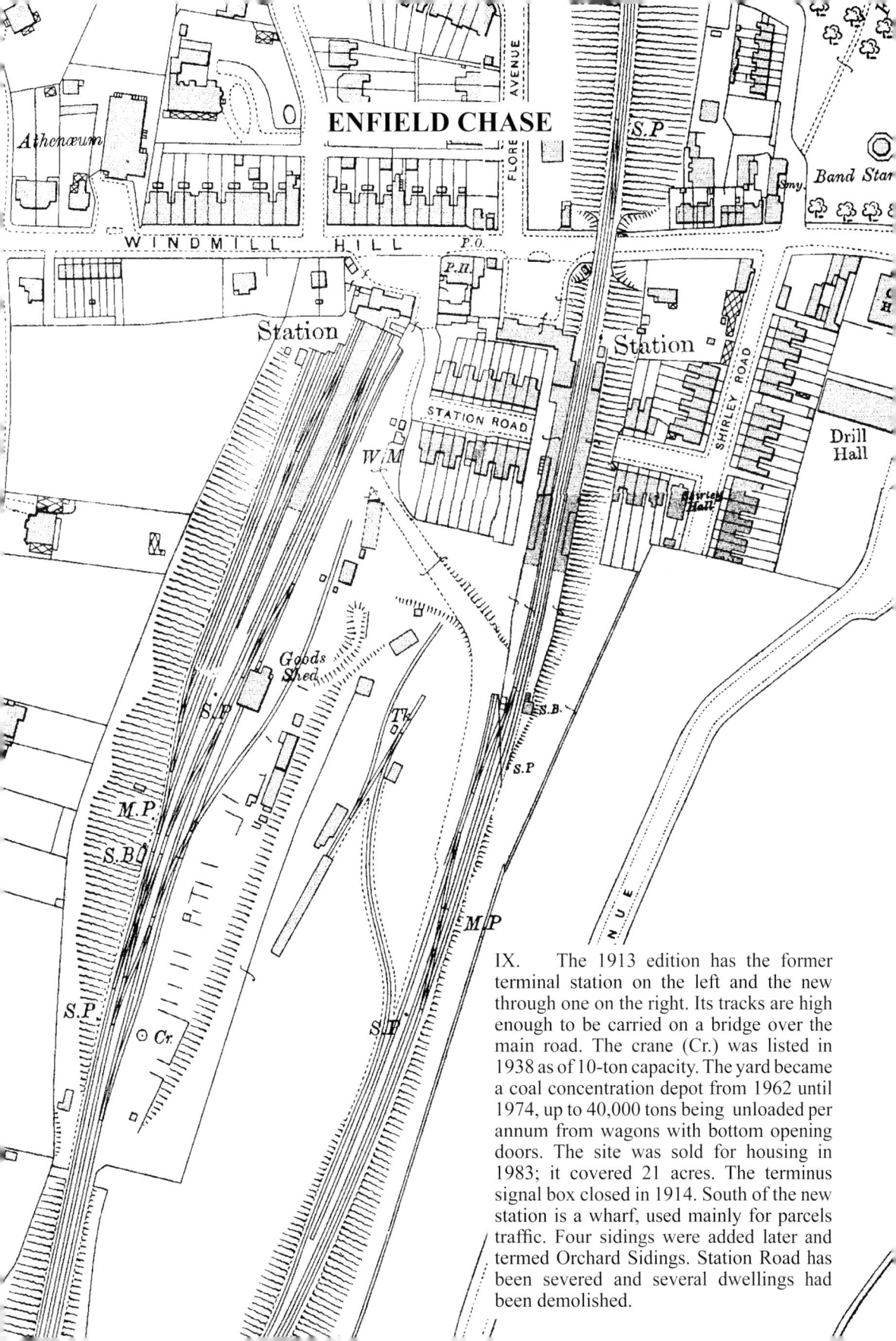

ENFIELD CHASE

(Map labels: Athenæum; Windmill Hill; P.O.; P.H.; Flore Avenue; Station Road; Shirley Road; Drill Hall; Band Stand; Station; Station; Goods Shed; W.M.; S.B.; S.P.; M.P.; Cr.; T; Avenue)

IX. The 1913 edition has the former terminal station on the left and the new through one on the right. Its tracks are high enough to be carried on a bridge over the main road. The crane (Cr.) was listed in 1938 as of 10-ton capacity. The yard became a coal concentration depot from 1962 until 1974, up to 40,000 tons being unloaded per annum from wagons with bottom opening doors. The site was sold for housing in 1983; it covered 21 acres. The terminus signal box closed in 1914. South of the new station is a wharf, used mainly for parcels traffic. Four sidings were added later and termed Orchard Sidings. Station Road has been severed and several dwellings had been demolished.

36. We start with two pictures of the first station of 1871. It had two platform faces made of sleepers initially. In 1883, a canopy was built supported with ornate tracery in the stanchion brackets. This is the view north towards the ticket barrier. (Lens of Sutton coll.)

37. Turning round, we see a train ready to depart and another in one of the two carriage sidings. The goods yard is on the left, together with the goods shed. Part of the canopy is at Whitewebbs Transport Museum in Enfield. Please also see picture 120. (Lens of Sutton coll.)

38. The north elevation of the 1910 station is seen soon after its opening. It became "Enfield Chase" on 1st July 1923, after becoming part of the LNER. Chase referred to hunting grounds. (Lens of Sutton coll.)

39. We proceed up the stairs and look south along the new wooden platforms to the signal box. This had a 25-lever frame and functioned from 4th April 1910 until 3rd September 1972. (Lens of Sutton coll.)

40. A view north in about 1960 reveals that little had changed. Sunday morning trains from London terminated at Gordon Hill in that period. (Lens of Sutton coll.)

41. The 10.45 service from Letchworth to Moorgate arrives on 22nd June 1987, formed of no. 313042. The train fleet depot is at Hornsey, but some are berthed at Letchworth and also Welwyn Garden City. (B.Morrison)

42. Forming the 11.23 service from Hertford to King's Cross, no. 317350 rounds the curve into Enfield Chase on 22nd June 1987. The bridge is over the main street.
(B.Morrison)

43. No. 31458 hauls southbound vans through Enfield Chase on 22nd June 1987. The two-tone vehicle contained a guards compartment.
(B.Morrison)

44. The exterior had changed little when photographed on 4th August 1991. Network SouthEast red, white and blue livery was widely evident.
(B.W.L.Brooksbank)

GORDON HILL

X. This is regarded by many as the fringe of London's suburbia and the layout was designed for the termination of trains. Terraced housing is on the right of this 1913 map.

Gordon Hill Station
Allotment Gardens

Allotment Gardens

G.N.R. ENFIELD BRANCH EXTENSION

HILL

HOLTWHITE'S HILL

Joseph's Home

Nurseries

L.N.E.R.
2246
FOR CONDITIONS SEE BACK. Available for three days, including day of issue.
WINCHMORE HILL to BOWES PARK or GORDON HILL
Fare THIRD / $ \ 4d. N CLASS
2246

45.   There were no space constraints and so a generous station approach was provided, as was a large house for the stationmaster, right. (Lens of Sutton coll.)

46.   A view north from the up platform shows spacious provision for gentlemen and the surprising covering of the sleepers with ballast at such a late date. Accident inspectors had for long criticised this custom. (Lens of Sutton coll.)

47. A down express from King's Cross hauled by no. 60001 *Sir Ronald Matthews* passes through on a Sunday afternoon in the late 1950s. The train had been diverted because of engineering work on the main line. (S.Elkin)

48. Gas lighting with Sugg's Windsor style lamps was still to be enjoyed in the early 1960s. Terminating here on weekdays in that era was the 5.05pm from Broad Street and the 6.02 from King's Cross. (Lens of Sutton coll.)

49. Another view from the same period features the water tank necessary for locomotives terminating trains here. Also included is the 26-lever signal box, which was working until 4th July 1976. It had a panel from 1972. (Lens of Sutton coll.)

50. Diesel services started in 1958 with Cravens diesel multiple units on off-peak workings. This photograph shows a 4-car DMU on a summer Sunday afternoon in about 1960 on a train from Hertford North to King's Cross. In the background are locomotive hauled BR Mark 1 suburban coaches stabled in the up bay platform ready for the Monday morning peak hour services. Four sets of coaches were stabled overnight and at weekends (in the down siding and the up bay) for trains starting here. (S.Elkin)

51. Diverted because of engineering works on the main line on 18th February 1973, no. 5652 is working the 13.20 Cambridge to King's Cross and approaches the station. There is evidence of track alterations in progress. (R.Hummerston)

52. A photograph from September 1974 shows the structure to still be in good order and electric lighting to have arrived. (R.M.Casserley)

53. A view north in 1997 reveals the loss of the down canopy, but at least the footbridge still had roofing. The up bay was still in use. (F.Hornby)

54. No. 313048 is northbound on 14th January 1997 and on the right is one of the mirrors installed for driver-only train operation. (F.Hornby)

55.   Empty coaching stock formed of two 3-car class 313 electric multiple units enters the up bay at 09.30 on 15th May 2002, ready to work the 09.42 stopping train to King's Cross. The first unit is in Network SouthEast livery and the second is in WAGN plain white. This train was part of the emergency timetable following the Potters Bar derailment, although the up bay platform was used regularly for a few peak hour services. (R.Elkin)

56.   A down Hull Trains class 170 diesel multiple unit runs through on 15 May 2002. The train had been diverted following the disaster at Potters Bar. This was the first "Open Access" operator, not a franchisee. (R.Elkin)

57. EWS class 66 Co-Co diesel locomotive no. 66087 passes through in May 2002 with an up freight train carrying building blocks. (R.Elkin)

NORTH OF GORDON HILL

58. "Britannia" class 4-6-2 no. 70037 *Hereward the Wake* passes Golf Links Crossing between Gordon Hill and Crews Hill (known locally as Tingey Tops) on an express from Cleethorpes to King's Cross on a Sunday afternoon in about 1963. The train had been diverted because of engineering work on the main line. (R.Elkin)

59. Also diverted because of engineering works, is no. 47430. It is seen on 3rd March 1974, between Crews Hill and Gordon Hill, bound for King's Cross and alongside masts, which are evidence of forthcoming electrification. The train will soon pass over the 165 yd-long Rendlesham Viaduct. (R.Hummerston)

CREWS HILL

William's Farm

4 ft. R.H.

XI. The 1914 survey shows the layout of the goods yard to be similar to that at the next station north. There was a notable horse box traffic, but the yard closed on 1st October 1962.

Crews Hill Station

60. CREWS HILL LNER is proudly laid out behind the oil lamps. All had to go with the advent of war, when station names were simply called out. (D.Cockle coll.)

61. A southward view in the 1960s includes a perforated concrete signal post near the road bridge. The horizontal and vertical white lines were added as an aid during the blackout of WWII. (Lens of Sutton coll.)

62. The original buildings were still to be seen on 17th September 1974. We are looking north and the crossover had long gone. The signal box on the map had 25 levers and closed on 3rd September 1972. (R.M.Casserley)

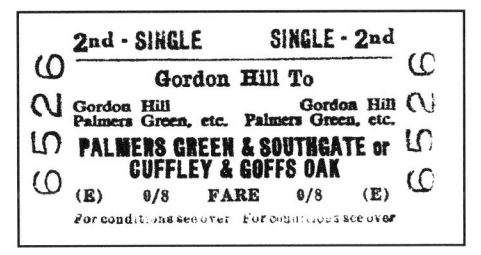

63.   The entrance was built on the east side of the line and was photographed on 25th June 1985. Corrugated iron was the cheapest cladding for buildings. (D.A.Thompson)

64.   The tunnel through the embankment was recorded on 14th January 1997. Five down trains on weekday evenings did not stop here. (F.Hornby)

CUFFLEY

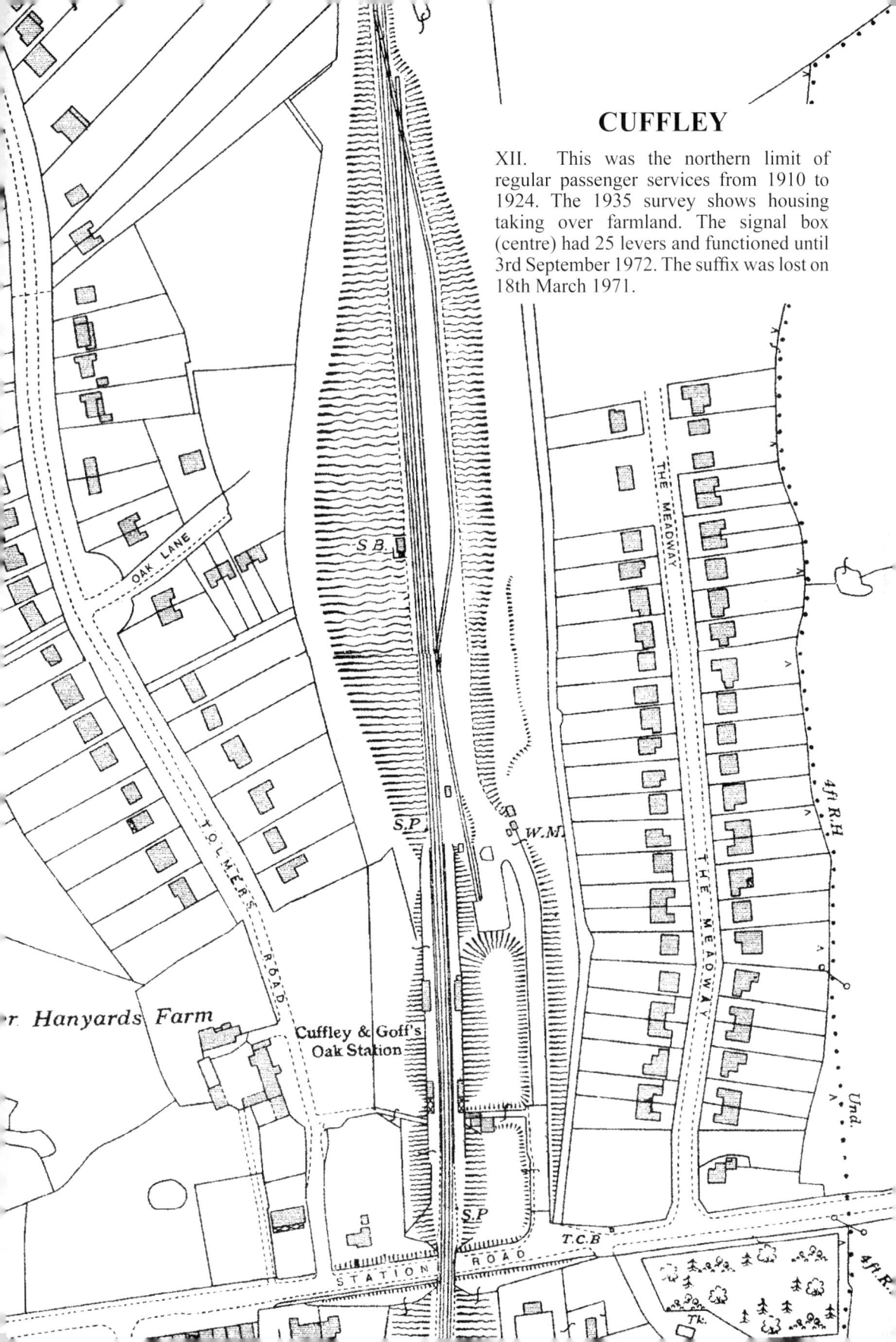

XII. This was the northern limit of regular passenger services from 1910 to 1924. The 1935 survey shows housing taking over farmland. The signal box (centre) had 25 levers and functioned until 3rd September 1972. The suffix was lost on 18th March 1971.

65.   Sadly no details were recorded of this 1909 view. It may involve hoisting the girders for the road bridge. A temporary standard gauge line was laid along the side of the full length of the construction site and was connected to the GNR at both ends. (P.Dace coll.)

66.   A poor newspaper photograph shows that crowds travelled from London in September 1916 to see the first German airship to be shot down in this country. A memorial in East Ridgeway marks the spot. (P.Dace coll.)

67. A rural cottage similar to that at Crews Hill was provided; the cover for the top flight of the stairs is included in this and the next view. (Lens of Sutton coll.)

68. Arriving on 15th November 1958 is class N2 0-6-2T no. 69585 with the 12.01pm Hertford North to King's Cross train. The locomotive lasted until September 1961. (D.T.Rowe)

69. Two views from the 1960s record the complete scene at that time. This northward panorama includes the goods yard, which closed on 1st October 1962. (Lens of Sutton coll.)

70. The bridge over Station Road is in the distance, as crowds gather for a train to London. On the right is the first aid cupboard, which contained a stretcher. (Lens of Sutton coll.)

71. A diverted King's Cross to Bradford express passes through on a Sunday evening in the mid-1960s, hauled by Brush Type 4 Co-Co diesel locomotive no. D1519. (R.Elkin)

72. The up side west elevation is visible in detail, together with the staff crossing and the lamp room. This was always remote from the main buildings for safety reasons. The goods yard in the distance was used to film a Castrol advertisement on 16th April 1966. This involved no. 4472 *Flying Scotsman* spinning its wheels on a film of oil! (Lens of Sutton coll.)

73. A northward view on 17th September 1974 includes the covers for both stairwells, plus the new electric lighting. (R.M.Casserley)

74. The entrance was photographed on the same day, along with the unassuming cycle shed. It is recorded that such premises were also suitable for courting. (R.M.Casserley)

75. No. 313027 is departing for London on 18th February 1998, with the Network SouthEast base-chilling red seats and an unmissable timepiece evident. (F.Hornby)

76. The iron sheds were replaced just before the NSE era with this symmetrical brick structure. It was recorded on 25th June 1985, along with the massive car park developed on the goods yard site. (D.A.Thompson)

NORTH OF CUFFLEY

77. Ponsbourne Tunnel is 1 mile 924 yards in length and much of the excavated clay was used to make the 30 million bricks needed to line it. Much London refuse was used to create the embankments on the route. (ICE)

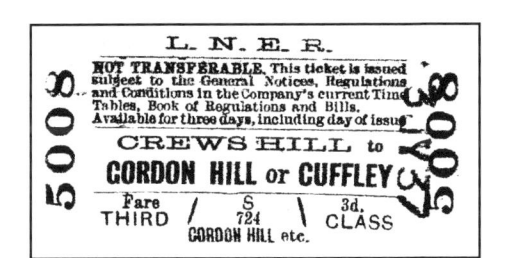

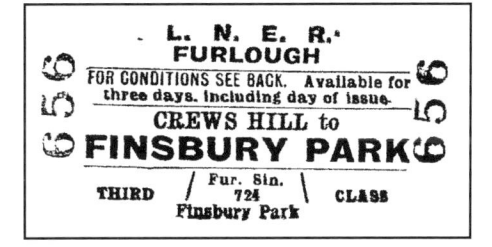

BAYFORD

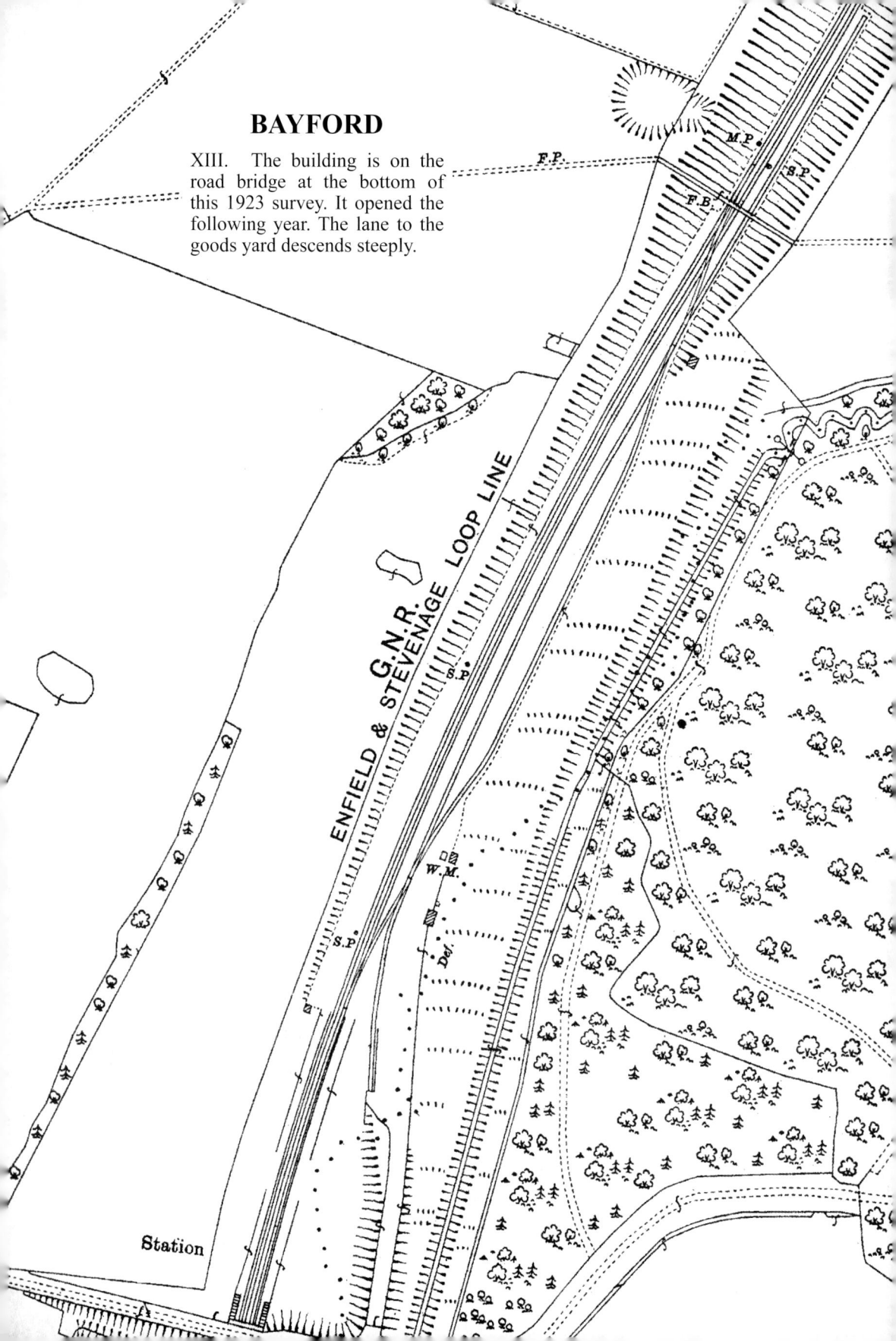

XIII. The building is on the road bridge at the bottom of this 1923 survey. It opened the following year. The lane to the goods yard descends steeply.

ENFIELD & STEVENAGE LOOP LINE G.N.R.

Station

78. An AEC bus provides alternative transport, while a Morris Minor and Morris Oxford enhance this nostalgic scene from the 1960s. The station was the least used on the route south of Hertford. (Lens of Sutton coll.)

79. The goods traffic was also small and so the yard was sometimes used for stock storage. This northward panorama is from 5th February 1961. The government held emergency stocks of paper here during WWII, in case Fleet Street was destroyed. (B.W.L.Brooksbank)

80. No. D5642 is running through with empty coaching stock on 12th May 1968. On the right is the overgrown goods yard, which had closed on 1st October 1962. (R.Hummerston)

81. After the advent of continuous welded rails and electrification, there was little change to the local scene. It is pictured on 17th September 1974. All trains stopped here by that time, except some at night and two rush hour trains to Broad Street on weekday mornings. (R.M.Casserley)

82. There was a box adjacent to milepost 17, with five levers until 3rd September 1972. It was called Bayford Block Hut and had latterly been used only at peak times. (D.Cockle)

83. The rural location and tiny dimensions are emphasised in this record from 28th November 1983. On Sundays, alternate trains did not call here. The ticket office was burnt out in 1991 and not replaced. (D.A.Thompson)

SOUTH OF HERTFORD NORTH

84. A class N2 0-6-2T heads south in the early 1950s and passes over the Hatfield branch on Hertford Viaduct. (A.Dudman)

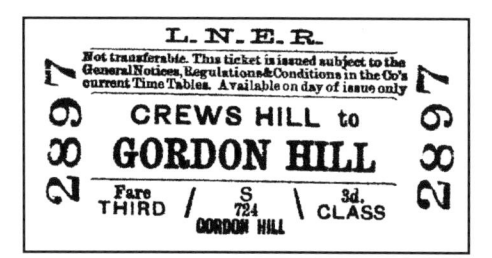

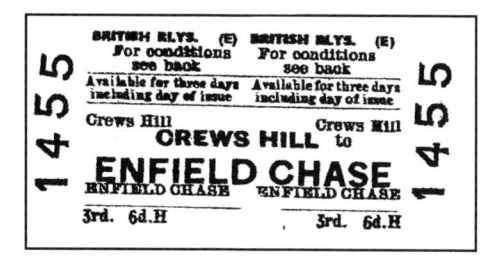

HERTFORD NORTH

XIV. The 1938 map at 6ins to 1 mile has our route close to the left border, with the single line from Hatfield curving in on the left and passing under it. The branch passes through Hertford North and runs across the top of the town. Its terminus is marked as **Station**, although not used as such for 14 years. Hertford East is on the right, together with the ex-GER line from Broxbourne.

For other views of this station, also the routes east and west, please see our *Branch Lines around Hertford and Hatfield* album.

85. The station was built partly in cutting and partly on embankment. The platforms on the latter were built on concrete arches on concrete piers. (ICE)

86. This view from the south includes new platforms and the single line used for freight traffic in the period 1918-24. On the right is the Hatfield branch which was not connected at that time. (ICE)

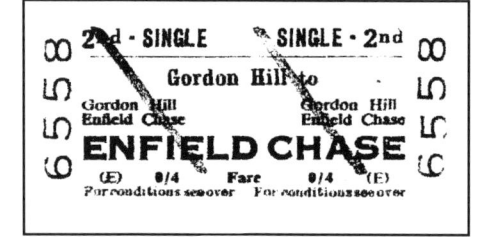

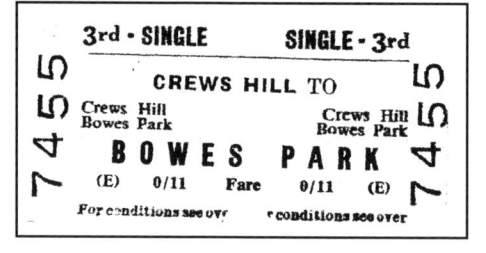

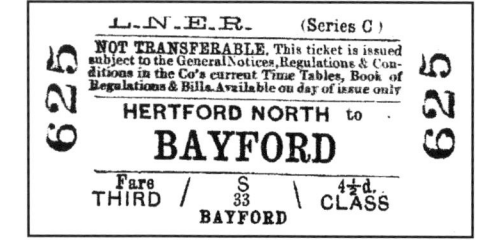

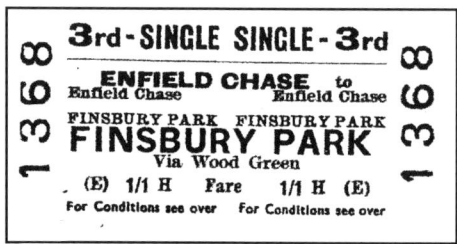

87. Ex-GNR railmotor no. 5 with the body in LNER livery stands on the down line. The driver will be at the right of the unit on its journey to Hitchin in July 1924. (A.Dudman coll.)

88. It is 7.40am on 13th September 1953 and the main line was closed and so class A2 4-6-2 no. 60506 *Wolf of Badenoch* appears from the mist with a sleeping car express from Scotland. (D.T.Rowe)

89. Class L1 2-6-4T no. 67774 waits to leave for London in the late 1950s. This and the adjacent platform were used for all scheduled passenger trains at this period, as none ran northwards. The platform on the right never received track. (R.S.Carpenter)

90. We now have a view from the early 1960s. The up platform is on the left and is devoid of shelter and white edging, as it seldom saw a passenger. The lift on the right linked with the subway for parcel traffic. The town grew from 9322 in 1901 to 17,290 in 1961. (Lens of Sutton coll.)

91. No. D5624 slid on icy rails in the early morning of 18th February 1971 and nearly ruined the rhubarb bed near North Road. It had been on its way to heat three sets of coaches using a special hose with two branches. (D.Cockle)

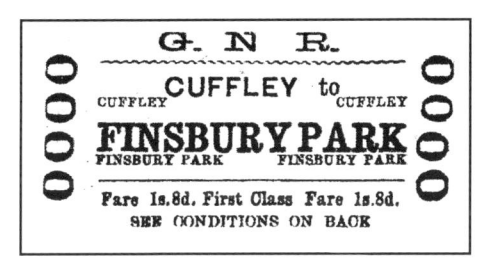

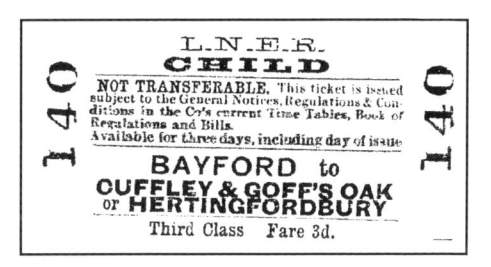

92. No. D5606 is approaching its destination with the 17.35 King's Cross to Hertford North on 9th September 1971. It has just passed over Hornsmill Viaduct and Hertford Viaduct. They have seven and 20 arches respectively; the latter has a steel span as well. The Hatfield line had been behind the signal box. (R.Hummerston)

93. Having arrived minutes later with evening peak services from London and stabled their respective stock, no. D5606 (leading) and no. D5590 await the road for their return journey on the same day. (R.Hummerston)

94. Seen from the footbridge in May 1974 are naked masts and a wiring train hauled by no. 31248. The leading vehicle is an ex-Southern Railway eight-wheeled brake van. (N.L.Cadge)

95. Hertford is near the clock and Langley Junction is on the right of the diagram. This panel replaced the 65-lever frame on 18th July 1971, but the clock was retained, as was the old building. The box was closed on the 4th July 1976 and control passed to King's Cross. Dave Cockle is on duty. (N.L.Cadge)

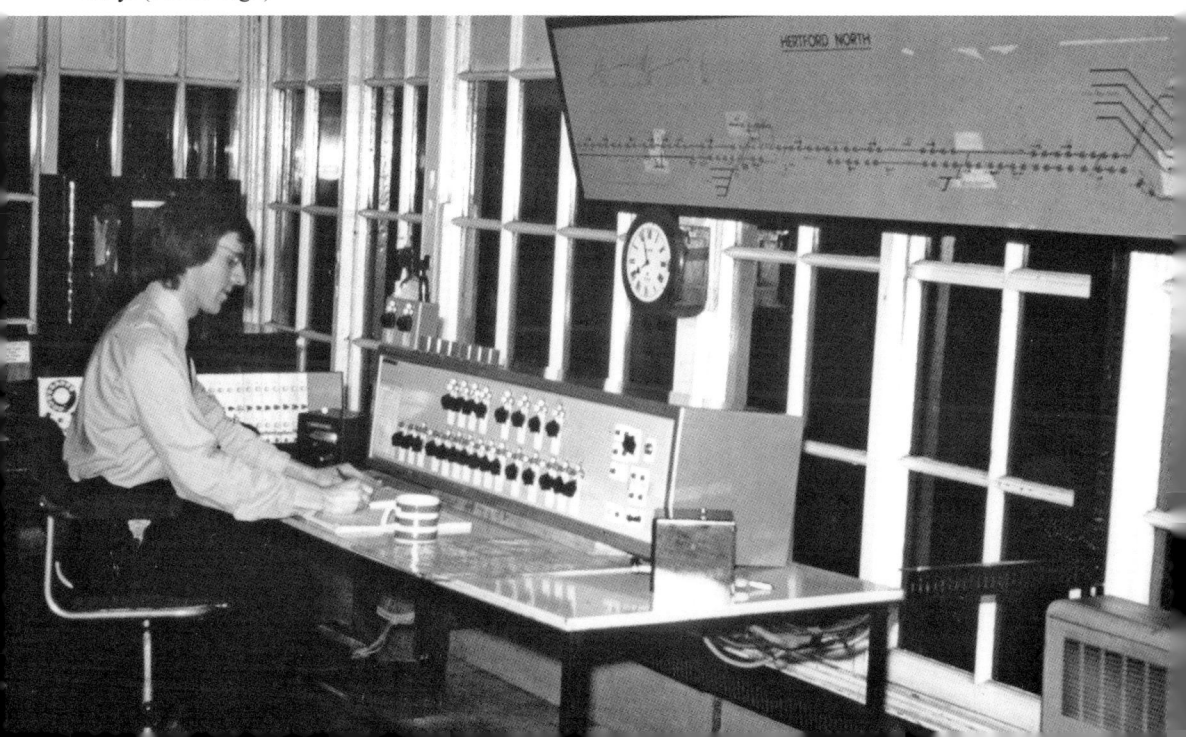

96. Trains began to call again regularly at the up platform (right) in 1962. By the time that this photograph was taken in September 1974, it had received a fence along the edge that had never been used. (H.C.Casserley)

97. The entrance was recorded on 25th June 1985. The parcel subway was level with the ticket office and the passenger subway was at a higher level, access being up a flight of steps. The remoteness of the station from the town centre has always been unpopular. On the left is an abutment of the bridge which once carried trains from the west to Hertford town. (D.A.Thompson)

98. The three platforms accommodate seven coaches each. No. 317661 arrives at its destination on 20th December 1998, forming the 09.34 WAGN service from King's Cross. This is the rear of the train. (B.Morrison)

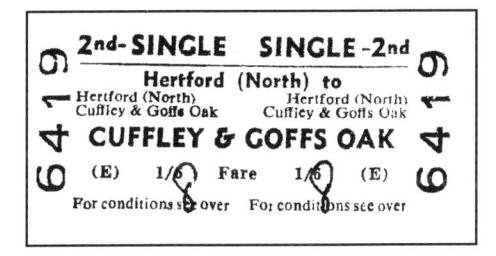

99. The bridge is seen in picture 93 and carries only a footpath. The diverted 08.40 King's Lynn to King's Cross service on 20th December 1998, passes Hertford North, formed of no. 365529. (B.Morrison)

100. Four electrified berthing sidings were laid on the up side of the running lines, south of the station. They were designed for ten 3-car units and three of four cars. The Hatfield branch had earlier descended on the left. "The Royal Sovereign" charter, the 09.28 from King's Cross to Norwich, passes them on 20th December 1998, powered by 'King' class 4-6-0 no. 6024 *King Edward I*. (B.Morrison)

101. The station entrance was rebuilt and came into use in 1990. The lower subway provided step-free access to the down platforms. The new booking hall was photographed from the high level subway on 8th August 2009. (B.W.L.Brooksbank)

NORTH OF HERTFORD

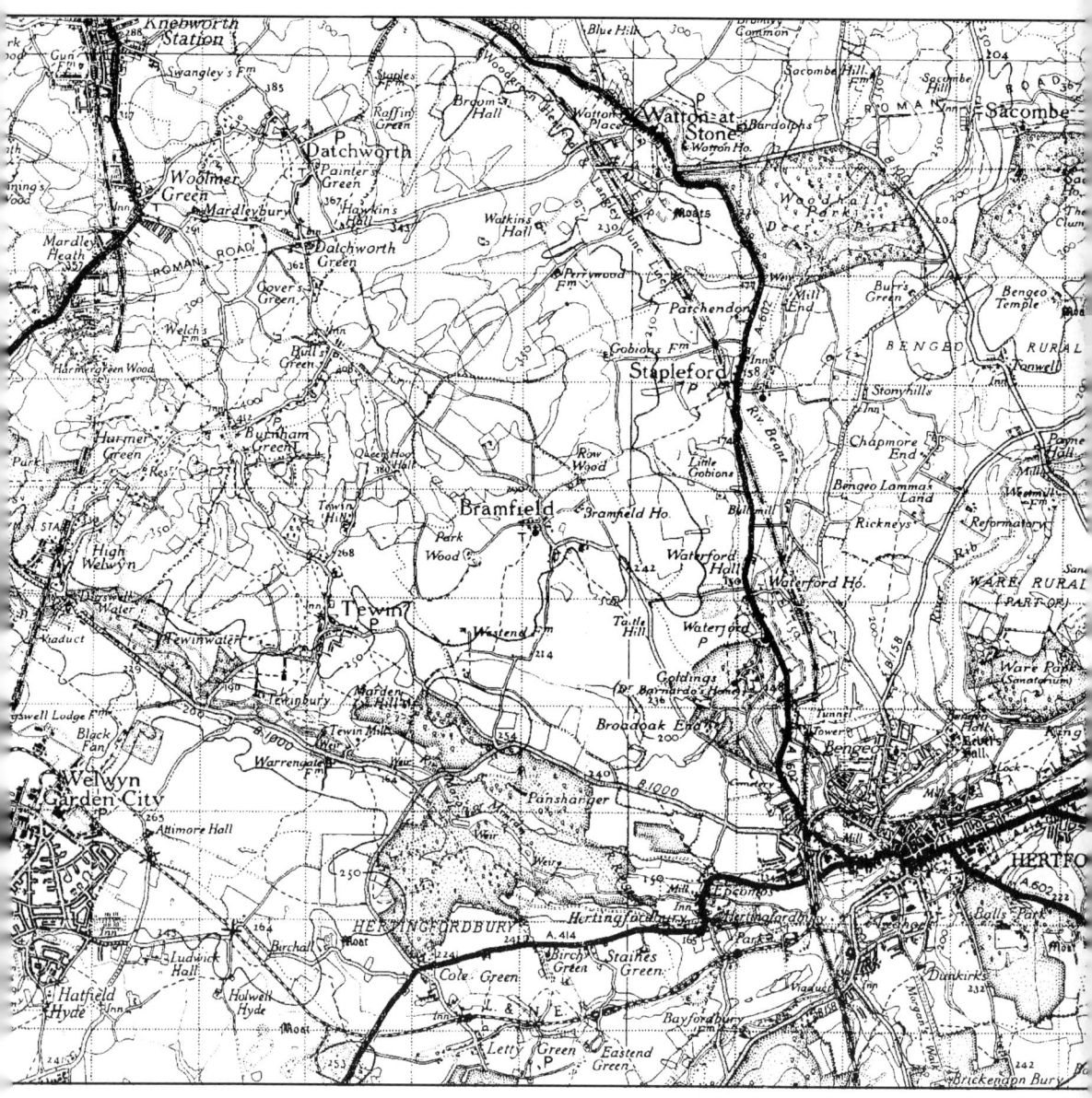

XV. The 1945 survey at 1ins to 1 mile has the Hatfield branch across the bottom and the double track to Broxbourne on the right. North of Hertford is the 364yd long Molewood Tunnel. Its up line was sometimes used during WWII to berth the Royal Train at night, when it was occupied by the monarch.

102.   A Cravens 4-car DMU forms an up local service from Peterborough and passes Waterford on 4th September 1971. This is about two miles north of Hertford, see map. The severed siding on the right was for Waterford Sand Pit. (R.Hummerston)

103.   This bridge was east of Waterford and was from where the previous photograph was taken. It is curious that a bridge built in the 20th century should have such a low limit. A substantial bridge with 43-ton girders was built over the Great North Road (A602 from 1919) north of Hertford. (R.Hummerston)

STAPLEFORD

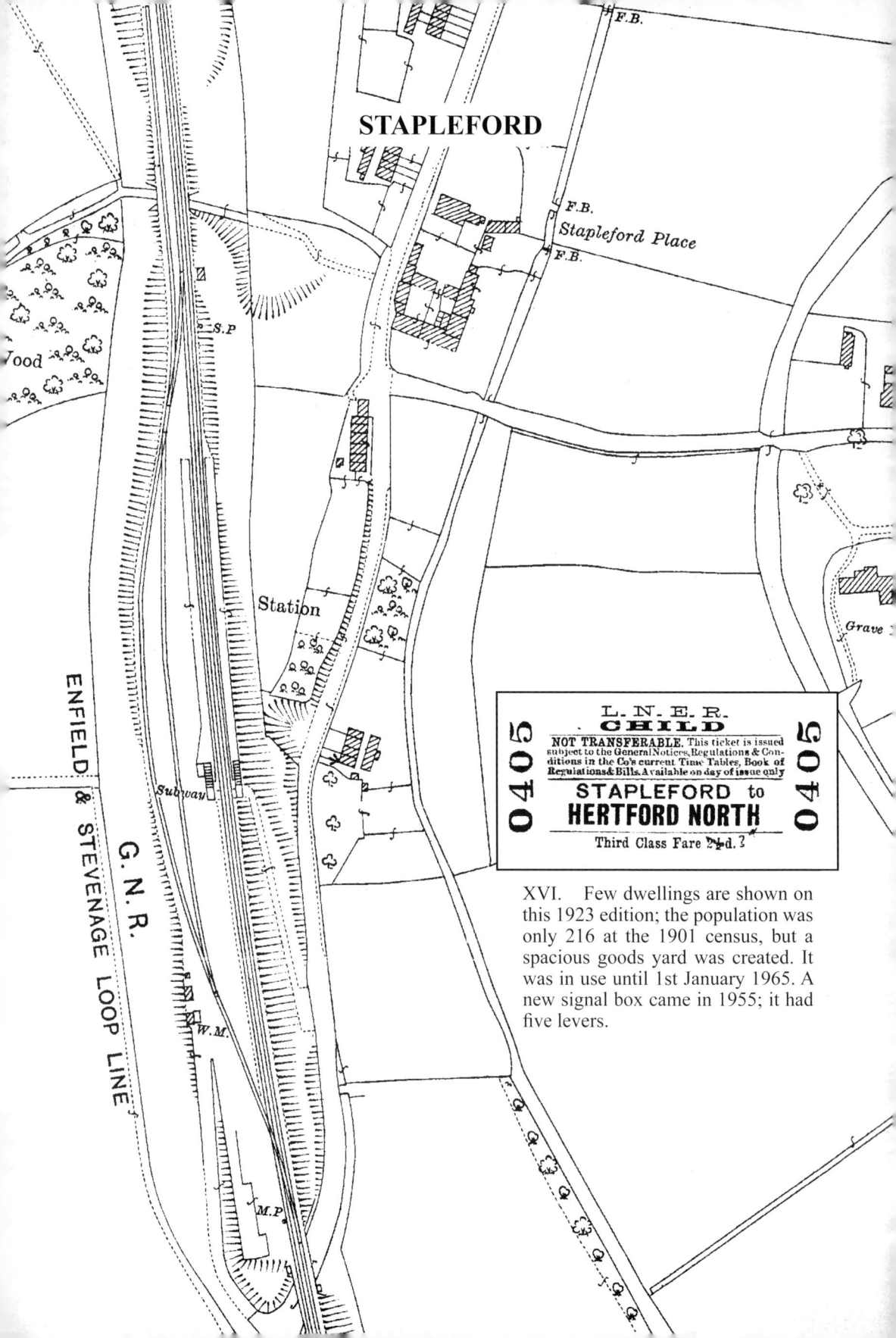

Stapleford Place

Station

Subway

ENFIELD & STEVENAGE LOOP LINE

G.N.R.

| L.N.E.R. |
| CHILD |
| NOT TRANSFERABLE. This ticket is issued subject to the General Notices, Regulations & Conditions in the Co's current Time Tables, Book of Regulations & Bills. Available on day of issue only |
| STAPLEFORD to **HERTFORD NORTH** |
| Third Class Fare 2½d. ? |

0405   0405

XVI. Few dwellings are shown on this 1923 edition; the population was only 216 at the 1901 census, but a spacious goods yard was created. It was in use until 1st January 1965. A new signal box came in 1955; it had five levers.

104. Class A3 4-6-2 no. 4472 *Flying Scotsman* was photographed standing with the "Flying Scotsman" sometime in 1929. It appears to be running "wrong road" through the station; the circumstances were the making of the film called "The Flying Scotsman"; it became Britain's third "talkie" in 1930. The camera is on the flat wagon. (LNER)

105. The trial of an AEC Regal railcoach destined for Havana took place in 1933. Temporary turntables were installed in sidings here and at Hertford North. Speeds of 50mph and petrol consumption of 6mpg were recorded. It was fitted with 38 seats, four sanders and one starting handle. A competitive vehicle can be seen in picture 45 in *Branch Lines around Towcester*. (AEC)

106. Class K3 2-6-0 no. 61929 heads a diverted London bound fish train on 13th September 1953. Part of the signal box is visible behind the locomotive. The station closed to passengers on 10th September 1939 and never reopened. (D.T.Rowe)

WATTON-AT-STONE

XVII. The 6ins to 1 mile map of 1946 shows the station, although it was closed from 10th September 1939 until 17th May 1982. The population was 703 in 1901, this rising to 869 in 1961. A figure of 2000 to be served was quoted in 1982.

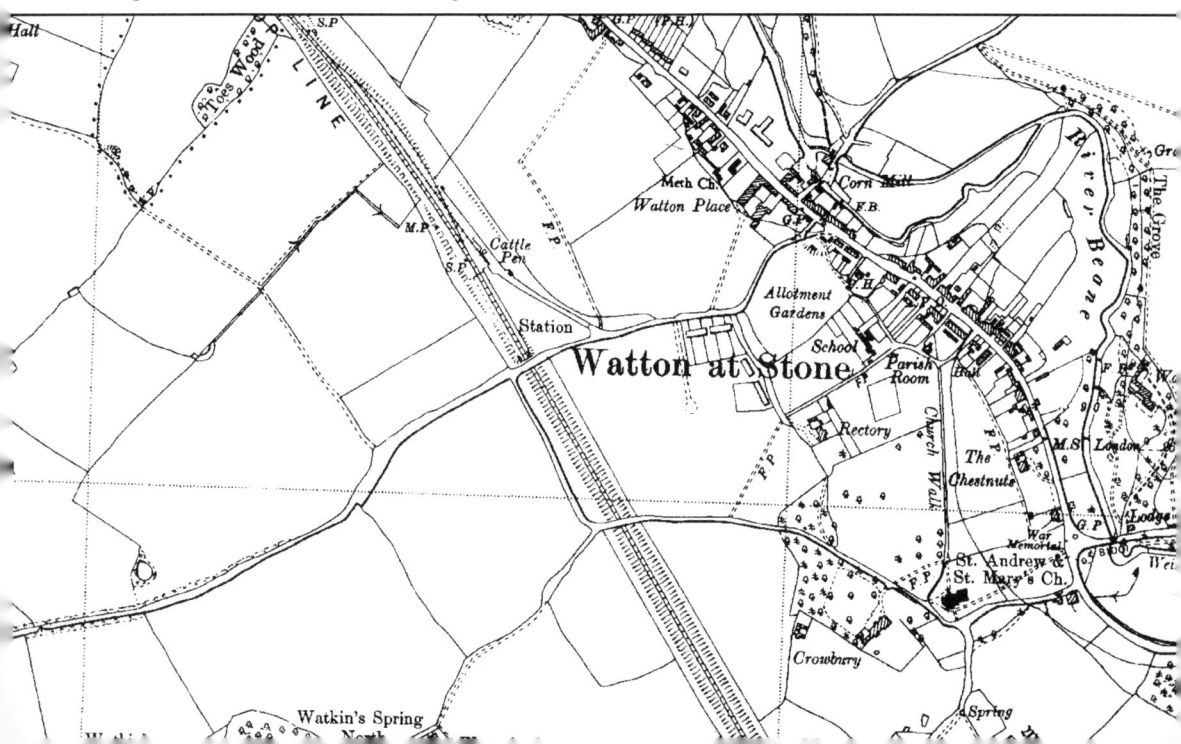

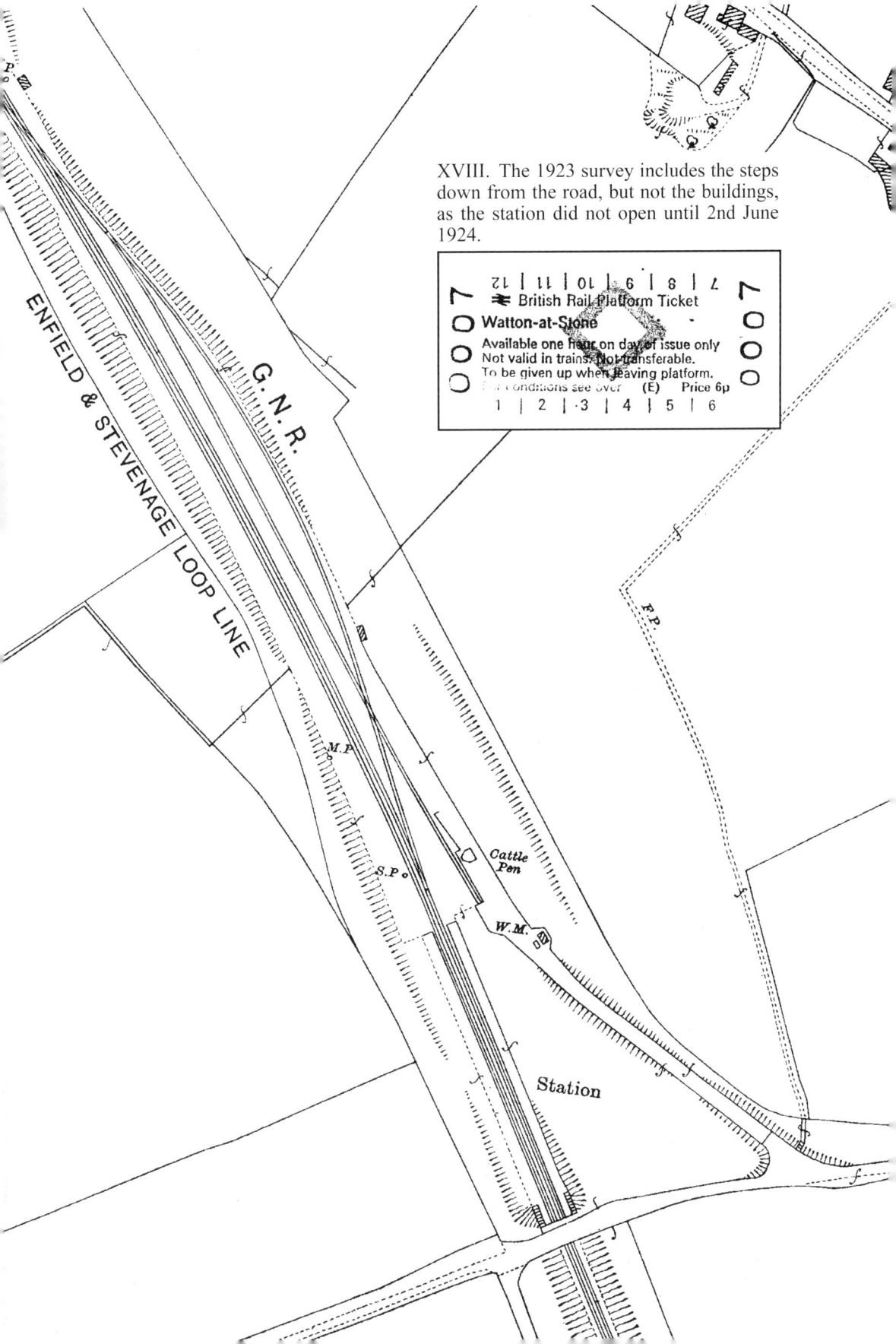

XVIII. The 1923 survey includes the steps down from the road, but not the buildings, as the station did not open until 2nd June 1924.

NEWS FLASH

on 17th MAY 1982
WATTON at STONE
will be re-opened to the public.

The new station stands on the site of the former station which was closed 43 years ago, and subsequently demolished.

The re-opening represents a triumph of successful co-operation between British Rail, the Hertfordshire County Council, and a number of District and Parish Councils.

The new station will serve the needs of a growing community, and will itself be served by through trains between London (Moorgate) and Letchworth. Full details of the train service are shown on the reverse.

It is your station — please use it.

HERTFORDSHIRE COUNTY COUNCIL

This is the age of the train ≷

Your new train service
until May 1983

To London (Moorgate)	To Letchworth
Mon-Sat	Mon-Sat
06.23	06.52
07.13 (SX)	07.22 (SX)
07.23 (SO)	07.52 (SO)
07b47 (SX)	08.02 (SX)
08.14 (SX)	08.22 (SO)
08.18 (SO)	08.43 (SX)
09.01 (SX)	09.22
09.18 (SO)	10.22
09.43 (SX)	Then at 22 mins past each hour until
10.18	
Then at 18 mins past each hour until	16e22 (SX)
	16.22 (SO)
16.18	16.42 (SX)
17.03 (SX)	17.17 (SX)
17.18 (SO)	17.22 (SO)
17.43 (SX)	17.53 (SX)
18.02 (SX)	18.22 (SO)
18.18 (SO)	18.24 (SX)
18.59 (SX)	18.55 (SX)
19.16 (SO)	19.22
19.41 (SX)	20.22
20.41	21.22
21.41	22.49
22.41	00.19
23c41	

SX - Not Saturdays   SO - Saturdays only.

Sundays

07.59 and at 59 mins past each hour until 15.59 then 17.02 and at 02 mins past each hour until 23d02	08.11 and at 11 mins past each hour until 23.11

(b) does not call at Bayford or Crews Hill
(c) terminates Hertford North
(d) operates to London (King's Cross)
(e) terminates at Hitchin

107. The Railway Enthusiasts Club ran a train from Fenchurch Street to terminate here on 15th June 1957. It went via North Woolwich and Lea Bridge behind BR 2-6-4T no. 80135 to Palace Gates. (F.Hornby)

108. At Palace Gates, the "Saracens Head Railtour" continued over the freight connection that day behind ex-LNER class N2 0-6-2T no. 69594. It is standing in the goods yard, waiting to return. (J.Langford)

109. The suffix AT STONE was added quickly, in July 1924. (Herts) was added in August 1926, but was not used upon reopening in 1982. (Lens of Sutton coll.)

110. This and the previous picture were taken in the early 1960s and give a complete record of this isolated location. The hyphens in the name seem to have been added recently.
(Lens of Sutton coll.)

111. The 14.45 service from King's Cross to Royston restarts from Watton-at-Stone on 6th September 1987, formed of no. 317361. The T refers to the termination of a temporary speed restriction. The train will soon use the flyunder at Langley Junction. (B.Morrison)

112. The diverted 12.11 (Sunday) HST from Harrogate to King's Cross passes Watton-at-Stone on 6th September 1987, with powercar no. 43111 leading. The oil terminal was owned by Cory's and was used from the 1960s to 80s. (B.Morrison)

113.   Basic platform facilities were provided for the reopening and are seen on 22nd November 1983. Trains then called once an hour, daily, with one or two extra at peak hours. (D.A.Thompson)

114.   The ticket office was built east of the bridge to be convenient to the car park, which was created on the site of the goods yard. This had closed on 10th June 1965. Opening hours were 06.45 to 11.50 on Mondays to Fridays in 2010. (D.A.Thompson)

SOUTH OF STEVENAGE

115. The "Railway Engineer" magazine produced this annotated illustration of Langley Junction in 1920. We look north and see the new down line passing under the 1850 main line. There were watertroughs north of the junction in the steam era. (ICE)

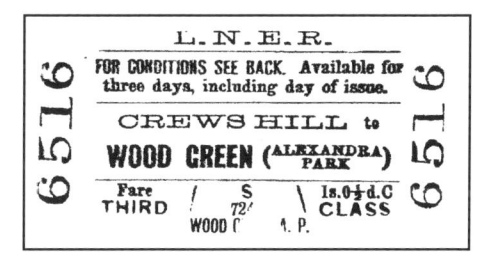

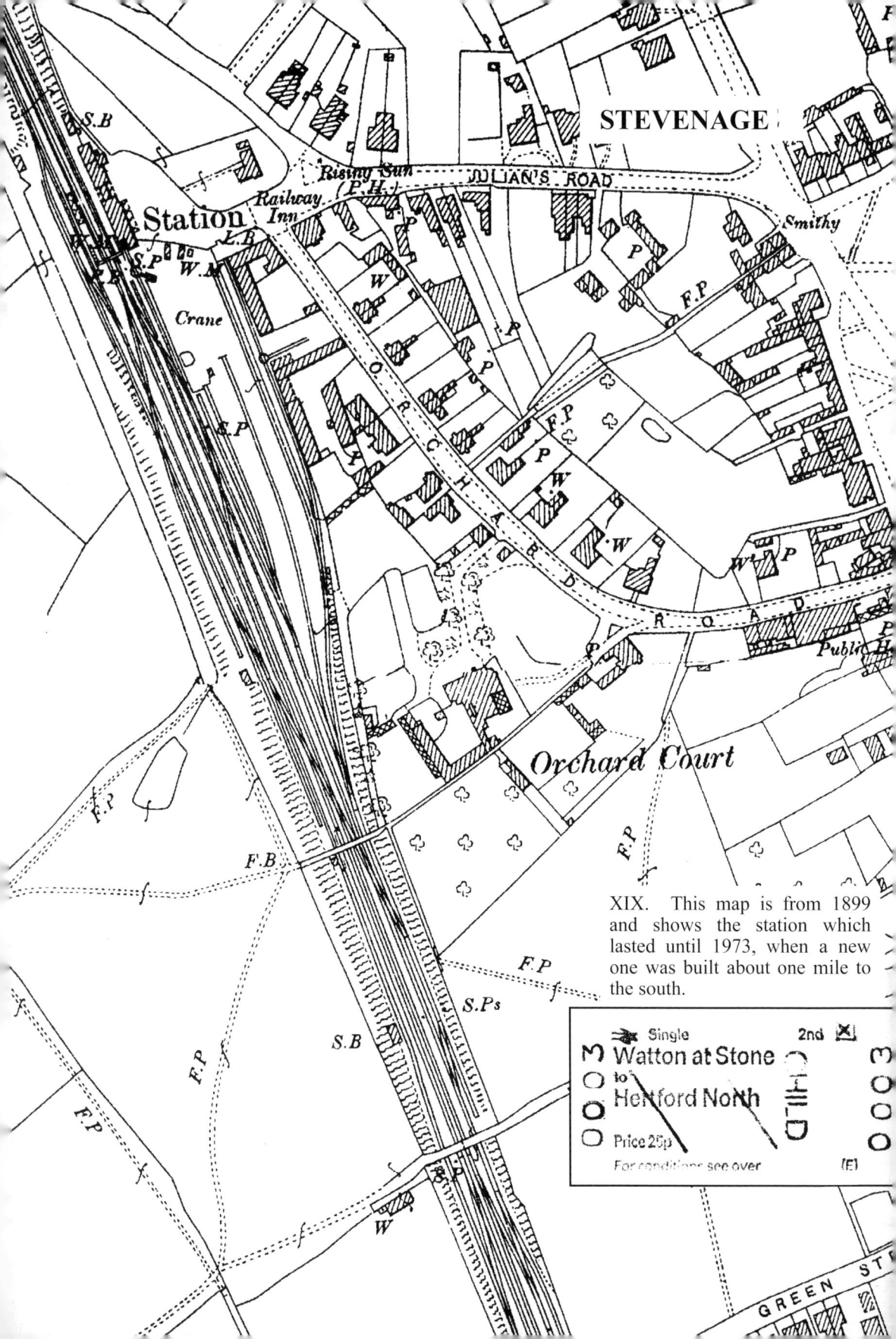

XIX. This map is from 1899 and shows the station which lasted until 1973, when a new one was built about one mile to the south.

116.   Only one photograph has been found to show the east elevation. This is the top floor of two and it was level with the footbridge. (Lens of Sutton coll.)

117.   The bridge at the north end of the two island platforms restricted signal sighting and thus each post had two co-acting arms. The lower ones are not visible in this view from the footbridge. (Lens of Sutton coll.)

118. Now for a view from the road bridge southwards, but missing is the main building, which is just beyond the left border, as is the goods yard. (Lens of Sutton coll.)

119. The new station opened on 23rd July 1973 and was designed with spacious features and easy access, plus copious car parking. (D.A.Thompson)

120. We end our journey, as many others do, at platform 4. No. 317340 is doing just that on 15th July 2005. Good buffets and good connections are available. (M.Turvey)

Other views of Stevenage can be enjoyed in the *Potters Bar to Cambridge* album.

POSTSCRIPT

121. Enfield goods depot was visited by a REC railtour on 26th August 1961. The platform canopy had been partially enclosed and bananas were unloaded under it. Beyond is part of the terminal building, but all has been lost. (D.Lawrence/H.Davies coll.)

MP Middleton Press
EVOLVING THE ULTIMATE RAIL ENCYCLOPEDIA

Easebourne Lane, Midhurst, West Sussex.
GU29 9AZ Tel:01730 813169
www.middletonpress.co.uk email:info@middletonpress.co.uk
A-978 0 906520 B- 978 1 873793 C- 978 1 901706 D-978 1 904474 E- 978 1 906008

All titles listed below were in print at time of publication - please check current availability by looking at our website - www.middletonpress.co.uk or by requesting a Brochure which includes our LATEST RAILWAY TITLES also our TRAMWAY, TROLLEYBUS, MILITARY and WATERWAYS series

A
Abergavenny to Merthyr C 91 8
Abertillery and Ebbw Vale Lines D 84 5
Allhallows - Branch Line to A 62 8
Alton - Branch Lines to A 11 6
Andover to Southampton A 82 6
Ascot - Branch Lines around A 64 2
Ashburton - Branch Line to B 95 4
Ashford - Steam to Eurostar B 67 1
Ashford to Dover A 48 2
Austrian Narrow Gauge D 04 3
Avonmouth - BL around D 42 5
Aylesbury to Rugby D 91 3

B
Baker Street to Uxbridge D 90 6
Banbury to Birmingham D 27 2
Banbury to Cheltenham E 63 5
Barking to Southend C 80 2
Barmouth to Pwllheli E 53 6
Barry - Branch Lines around D 50 0
Bath Green Park to Bristol C 36 9
Bath to Evercreech Junction A 60 4
Bedford to Wellingborough D 31 9
Birmingham to Wolverhampton E 25 3
Bletchley to Cambridge D 94 4
Bletchley to Rugby E 07 9
Bodmin - Branch Lines around B 83 1
Bournemouth & Poole Trys B 47 3
Bournemouth to Evercreech Jn A 46 8
Bournemouth to Weymouth A 57 4
Brecon to Neath D 43 2
Brecon to Newport D 16 6
Brecon to Newtown E 06 2
Brighton to Eastbourne A 16 1
Brighton to Worthing A 03 1
Bromley South to Rochester B 23 7
Bromsgrove to Birmingham D 87 6
Bromsgrove to Gloucester D 73 9
Brunel - A railtour of his achievements D 74 2
Bude - Branch Line to B 29 9
Burnham to Evercreech Junction B 68 0

C
Cambridge to Ely D 55 5
Canterbury - Branch Lines around B 58 9
Cardiff to Dowlais (Cae Harris) E 47 5
Cardiff to Swansea E 42 0
Carmarthen to Fishguard E 66 6
Caterham & Tattenham Corner B 25 1
Chard and Yeovil - BLs around C 30 7
Charing Cross to Dartford A 75 8
Charing Cross to Orpington A 96 3
Cheddar - Branch Line to B 90 9
Cheltenham to Andover C 43 7
Cheltenham to Redditch D 81 4
Chichester to Portsmouth A 14 7
Clapham Junction to Beckenham Jn B 36 7
Cleobury Mortimer - BLs around E 18 5
Clevedon & Portishead - BLs to D 18 0
Colonel Stephens D 62 3
Consett to South Shields E 57 4
Cornwall Narrow Gauge D 56 2
Corris and Vale of Rheidol E 65 9
Craven Arms to Llandeilo E 35 2
Craven Arms to Wellington E 33 8
Crawley to Littlehampton A 34 5
Cromer - Branch Lines around C 26 0
Croydon to East Grinstead B 48 0
Crystal Palace and Catford Loop B 87 1
Cyprus Narrow Gauge E 13 0

D
Darlington - Leamside - Newcastle E 28 4
Darlington to Newcastle D 98 2
Dartford to Sittingbourne B 34 3
Derwent Valley - Branch Line to the D 06 7
Devon Narrow Gauge E 09 3
Didcot to Banbury D 02 9
Didcot to Swindon C 84 0
Didcot to Winchester C 13 0
Dorset & Somerset Narrow Gauge D 76 0
Douglas to Peel C 88 8
Douglas to Port Erin C 55 0
Douglas to Ramsey D 39 5
Dover to Ramsgate A 78 9
Dublin Northwards in the 1950s E 31 4
Dunstable - Branch Lines to E 27 7

E
Ealing to Slough C 42 0
East Cornwall Mineral Railways D 22 7
East Croydon to Three Bridges A 53 6
Eastern Spain Narrow Gauge E 56 7
East Grinstead - Branch Lines to A 07 9
East London - Branch Lines of C 44 4
East London Line B 80 0
East of Norwich - Branch Lines E 69 7
Effingham Junction - BLs around A 74 1
Ely to Norwich C 90 1
Enfield Town & Palace Gates - BL to D 32 6
Epsom to Horsham A 30 7
Eritrean Narrow Gauge E 38 3
Euston to Harrow & Wealdstone C 89 5
Exeter to Barnstaple B 15 2
Exeter to Newton Abbot C 49 9
Exeter to Tavistock B 69 5
Exmouth - Branch Lines to B 00 8

F
Fairford - Branch Line to A 52 9
Falmouth, Helston & St. Ives - BL to C 74 1
Fareham to Salisbury A 67 3
Faversham to Dover B 05 3
Felixstowe & Aldeburgh - BL to D 20 3
Fenchurch Street to Barking C 20 8
Festiniog - 50 yrs of enterprise C 83 3
Festiniog 1946-55 E 01 7
Festiniog in the Fifties B 68 8
Festiniog in the Sixties B 91 6
Finsbury Park to Alexandra Palace C 02 8
Frome to Bristol B 77 0

G
Gloucester to Bristol D 35 7
Gloucester to Cardiff D 66 1
Gosport - Branch Lines around A 36 9
Greece Narrow Gauge D 72 2

H
Hampshire Narrow Gauge D 36 4
Harrow to Watford D 14 2
Hastings to Ashford A 37 6
Hawkhurst - Branch Line to A 66 6
Hayling - Branch Line to A 12 3
Hay-on-Wye - Branch Lines around D 92 0
Haywards Heath to Seaford A 28 4
Hemel Hempstead - Branch Lines to D 88 3
Henley, Windsor & Marlow - BL to C77 2
Hereford to Newport D 54 8
Hertford and Hatfield - BLs around E 58 1 6
Hertford Loop E 71 0
Hexham to Carlisle D 75 3
Hitchin to Peterborough D 07 4
Holborn Viaduct to Lewisham A 81 9
Horsham - Branch Lines A 02 4
Huntingdon - Branch Line to A 93 2

I
Ilford to Shenfield C 97 0
Ilfracombe - Branch Line to B 21 3
Industrial Rlys of the South East A 09 3
Ipswich to Saxmundham C 41 3
Isle of Wight Lines - 50 yrs C 12 3

K
Kent Narrow Gauge C 45 1
Kidderminster to Shrewsbury E 10 9
Kingsbridge - Branch Line to C 98 7
Kings Cross to Potters Bar E 62 8
Kingston & Hounslow Loops A 83 3
Kingswear - Branch Line to C 17 8

L
Lambourn - Branch Line to C 70 3
Launceston & Princetown - BL to C 19 2
Lewisham to Dartford A 92 5
Lines around Wimbledon B 75 6
Liverpool Street to Chingford D 01 2
Liverpool Street to Ilford C 34 5
Llandeilo to Swansea E 46 8
London Bridge to Addiscombe B 20 6
London Bridge to East Croydon A 58 1
Longmoor - Branch Lines to A 41 3
Looe - Branch Line to C 22 2
Lowestoft - Branch Lines around E 40 6
Ludlow to Hereford E 14 7
Lydney - Branch Lines around E 26 0
Lyme Regis - Branch Line to A 45 1
Lynton - Branch Line to B 04 6

M
Machynlleth to Barmouth E 54 3
March - Branch Lines around B 09 1
Marylebone to Rickmansworth D 49 4
Melton Constable to Yarmouth Beach E 03 1
Mexborough to Swinton E 36 9
Midhurst - Branch Lines around A 49 9
Mitcham Junction Lines B 01 5
Mitchell & company C 59 8
Monmouth - Branch Lines to E 20 8
Monmouthshire Eastern Valleys D 71 5
Moretonhampstead - BL to C 27 7
Moreton-in-Marsh to Worcester D 26 5
Mountain Ash to Neath D 80 7

N
Newbury to Westbury C 66 6
Newcastle to Hexham D 69 2
Newport (IOW) - Branch Lines to A 26 0
Newquay - Branch Lines to C 71 0
Newton Abbot to Plymouth C 60 4
Newtown to Aberystwyth E 41 3
North East German Narrow Gauge D 44 9
Northern France Narrow Gauge C 75 8
North London Line B 94 7
North Woolwich - BLs around C 65 9

O
Ongar - Branch Line to E 05 5
Oswestry - Branch Lines around E 60 4
Oxford to Bletchley D 57 9
Oxford to Moreton-in-Marsh D 15 9

P
Paddington to Ealing C 37 6
Paddington to Princes Risborough C 81 9
Padstow - Branch Line to B 54 1
Peterborough to Kings Lynn E 32 1
Plymouth - BLs around B 98 5
Plymouth to. St. Austell C 63 5
Pontypool to Mountain Ash D 65 4
Porthmadog 1954-94 - BL around B 31 2
Portmadoc 1923-46 - BL around B 13 8
Portsmouth to Southampton A 31 4
Portugal Narrow Gauge E 67 3
Potters Bar to Cambridge D 70 8
Princes Risborough - Branch Lines to D 05 0
Princes Risborough to Banbury C 85 7

R
Reading to Basingstoke B 27 5
Reading to Didcot C 79 6
Reading to Guildford A 47 5
Redhill to Ashford A 73 4
Return to Blaenau 1970-82 C 64 2
Rhymney and New Tredegar Lines E 48 2
Rickmansworth to Aylesbury D 61 6
Romania & Bulgaria Narrow Gauge E 23 9
Romneyrail C 32 1
Ross-on-Wye - Branch Lines around E 30 7
Rugby to Birmingham E 37 6
Ryde to Ventnor A 19 2

S
Salisbury to Westbury B 39 8
Saxmundham to Yarmouth C 69 7
Saxony Narrow Gauge D 47 0
Seaton & Sidmouth - Branch Lines to A 95 6
Selsey - Branch Line to A 04 8
Sheerness - Branch Line to B 16 2
Shrewsbury - Branch Line to A 86 4
Shrewsbury to Chester E 70 3
Shrewsbury to Ludlow E 21 5
Shrewsbury to Newtown E 29 1
Sierra Leone Narrow Gauge D 28 9
Sirhowy Valley Line E 12 3
Sittingbourne to Ramsgate A 90 1
Slough to Newbury C 56 7
South African Two-foot gauge E 51 2
Southampton to Bournemouth A 42 0
Southern France Narrow Gauge C 47 5
South London Line B 46 6
Southwold - Branch Line to A 15 4
Spalding - Branch Lines around E 52 9
St Albans to Bedford D 08 1
St. Austell to Penzance C 67 3
Steaming through the Isle of Wight A 56
Steaming through West Hants A 69 7
Stourbridge to Wolverhampton E 16 1
St. Pancras to Barking D 68 5
St. Pancras to St. Albans C 78 9
Stratford-upon-Avon to Birmingham D 77
Stratford-upon-Avon to Cheltenham C 25
Surrey Narrow Gauge C 87 1
Sussex Narrow Gauge C 68 0
Swanley to Ashford B 45 9
Swansea to Carmarthen E 59 8
Swindon to Bristol C 96 3
Swindon to Gloucester D 46 3
Swindon to Newport D 30 2
Swiss Narrow Gauge C 94 9

T
Talyllyn - 50 years C 39 0
Taunton to Barnstaple B 60 2
Taunton to Exeter C 82 6
Tavistock to Plymouth B 88 6
Tenterden - Branch Line to A 21 5
Three Bridges to Brighton A 35 2
Tilbury Loop C 86 4
Tiverton - Branch Lines around C 62 8
Tivetshall to Beccles D 41 8
Tonbridge to Hastings A 44 4
Torrington - Branch Lines to B 37 4
Towcester - Branch Lines around E 39 0
Tunbridge Wells - Branch Lines to A 32 1

U
Upwell - Branch Line to B 64 0

V
Victoria to Bromley South A 98 7
Vivarais Revisited E 08 6

W
Wantage - Branch Line to D 25 8
Wareham to Swanage - 50 yrs D 09 8
Waterloo to Windsor A 54 3
Waterloo to Woking A 38 3
Watford to Leighton Buzzard D 45 6
Welshpool to Llanfair E 49 9
Wenford Bridge to Fowey C 09 3
Westbury to Bath B 55 8
Westbury to Taunton C 76 5
West Cornwall Mineral Railways D 48 7
West Croydon to Epsom B 08 4
West German Narrow Gauge D 93 7
West London - Branch Lines of C 50 5
West London Line B 84 8
West Wiltshire - Branch Lines of D 12 8
Weymouth - Branch Lines around A 65 9
Willesden Junction to Richmond B 71 8
Wimbledon to Beckenham C 58 1
Wimbledon to Epsom B 62 6
Wimborne - Branch Lines around A 97 0
Wisbech 1800-1901 C 93 2
Wisbech - Branch Lines around C 01 7
Woking to Alton A 59 8
Woking to Portsmouth A 25 3
Woking to Southampton A 55 0
Wolverhampton to Shrewsbury E 44 4
Worcester to Birmingham D 97 5
Worcester to Hereford D 38 8
Worthing to Chichester A 06 2

Y
Yeovil - 50 yrs change C 38 3
Yeovil to Dorchester A 76 5
Yeovil to Exeter A 91 8